THE LIBRARY
ST. MARY'S COLLEGE OF MARYLAND
ST. MARY'S CITY, MARYLAND 20686

S0-FBR-587

Alejandro Casona

Twayne's World Authors Series
Spanish Literature

Janet Pérez, Editor
Texas Tech University

TWAS 748

ALEJANDRO CASONA
(1903–1965)
Photograph courtesy of Luis M. Rodríguez Sánchez and the Alejandro Casona estate

Alejandro Casona
By Harold K. Moon
Brigham Young University

Twayne Publishers • *Boston*

Alejandro Casona

Harold K. Moon

Copyright © 1985 by G. K. Hall & Company
All Rights Reserved
Published by Twayne Publishers
A Division of G. K. Hall & Company
70 Lincoln Street
Boston, Massachusetts 02111

Book Production by Elizabeth Todesco

Book Design by Barbara Anderson

Printed on permanent/durable acid-free
paper and bound in the United States of
America.

Library of Congress Cataloging in Publication Data

Moon, Harold K., 1934–
 Alejandro Casona.

 (Twayne's world authors series ; TWAS 748)
 Bibliography: p.
 Includes index.
  1. Casona, Alejandro, 1903–1965—Criticism and
interpretation. I. Title. II. Series.
PQ6633.O37Z7   1985   862'.62   84-15675
ISBN 0-8057-6596-4

Contents

About the Author
Preface
Chronology

Chapter One
Alejandro Casona: The Man and His Works 1

Chapter Two
Tradition's Legacy 27

Chapter Three
Fantasy versus Reality 76

Chapter Four
The Paranormal 97

Chapter Five
Historical Plays 105

Chapter Six
Summation 128

Notes and References 131
Selected Bibliography 141
Index 154

About the Author

Harold K. Moon is professor of Spanish at Brigham Young University. He completed the Ph.D. at Syracuse University in 1963. He has published numerous articles and books on nineteenth- and twentieth-century Spanish literature, including *Alejandro Casona, Playwright* (Provo: Merrill Monograph Series, Brigham Young University Press, 1970) and *Spanish Literature: A Critical Approach* (Lexington, Mass.: Xerox College Publishing, 1972). He has also published a volume of short stories (Provo: Merrill Monograph Series, Brigham Young University Press, 1982) and is currently completing two novels.

Preface

Critics have penned thousands of pages in censure of the sagging quality of Spain's dramatic output during this century. Among others, Azorín and Jacinto Grau stand out as they denounce the stagnation and artistic incest that characterize the earliest years. Another well-known critic, Juan Chabás, writing in 1934, echoes the same complaint. "A year of theater. An index of failures, incompetence, clumsiness," he grumbles. But he takes heart as he remembers the triumph of the two playwrights most capable of accomplishing for Spain a badly needed renovation: Federico García Lorca and Alejandro Casona.

To be sure, Alejandro Casona represents one of the brighter spots on this sometimes dismal horizon, and although much contemporary criticism does not favor him, the complaints are clearly ideological or politically motivated and not aesthetic. Constantino Suárez points out as indicative of Casona's international success that in May 1957 *La casa de los siete balcones* (The house of the seven gables) was playing in the Teatro Liceo in Buenos Aires, *Los árboles mueren de pie* (Trees die standing) in Belgrade, *Prohibido suicidarse en primavera* (No suicides in springtime) and *La tercera palabra* (The third word) in Belgium and Holland, *La dama del alba* (*The Lady of the Dawn*) in the Congo and at the Royal Theater in Athens, and *Corona de amor y muerte* (*Crown of Love and Death*) in Lisbon. Yet, ironically, his plays were for years banned and therefore scarcely known within his own homeland. In 1936, political pressures forced him out of his beloved Spain, but a year or two before his death, which occurred on September 17, 1965, he returned to put an end to his exile and to the obscurity in which his work had remained in his own country. So sweeping was his success that he surpassed all previous records in the number of plays presented simultaneously in the theaters throughout Spain and abroad.

It will be my aim in this study to follow Casona's theater through all of its optimism. Casona is not a writer of tragedy; his output belongs largely to the tradition of the "happy ending"

ALEJANDRO CASONA

(unforgivable in the modern, existential context!). His art is analyzed in light of his intent, the power of his dramatic insight, and his own thought and theories. His debt to tradition as well as his place in the modern currents of thought are examined, and I broach once again the familiar fantasy/reality theme, including the questions of solipsism and the paranormal, based on my own observations as well as all that has been written by others. And finally, as a category requiring its own approach, I examine Casona's historical plays, seeking to elucidate their characteristics and contributions.

Though Casona wrote poetry and essays, gave many lectures, and worked extensively in motion pictures, his most significant impact was in the theater. He saw himself as a playwright, and was not really comfortable when circumstances obliged him to ply his talents elsewhere. Therefore, as well as for limitations of space, this study will not cover his poetry or screenplays and will only deal with his essays to the degree that they contribute to the understanding of his theater; nor will it cover the works Casona produced in collaboration with other authors, none of which proved very successful.

An earlier study of mine, published but with very narrow distribution by the Charles E. Merrill Monograph Series in the Humanities and Social Sciences at Brigham Young University, serves as the point of departure for much of what I write here. I will be somewhat repetitive in that the present volume reiterates the essentials of this and of several relevant articles that I have written for various publications, some of very limited distribution, such as *Brigham Young University Studies.*

Translations, unless otherwise indicated, are my own.

Through the gestation of any book, the writer naturally incurs many debts of gratitude. My deep thanks to all who helped. But two names stand out more boldly than all the rest: Charles H. Leighton and the late Juan R. Castellano. My debt to Mr. Leighton goes back many years before this work was conceived, and readily I acknowledge that, but for him, it would not have been written. Nor would it have been possible without Mr. Castellano, who first inspired me to do the project.

Harold K. Moon

Brigham Young University

Chronology

1903 March 23: Alejandro Rodríguez Alvarez born in Besullo, a small village in Asturias, Spain.

1913 Begins studies leading to the baccalaureate, in Gijón, at the Instituto Jovellanos.

1919 Moves to Murcia, where he finishes the baccalaureate.

1919–1922 Enters the University of Murcia and collaborates in the publication of several magazines. A period of study and experimentation.

1922 Enrolls in the Escuela Superior del Magisterio in Madrid.

1926 Completes studies at the Superior; publishes his first book of poetry, *El peregrino de la barba florida* (The Pilgrim with the flowing beard), later disowned. Teaches in an elementary school in Madrid, completes a translation of Thomas De Quincey's *Confessions of an English Opium Eater,* and lectures on "The Life and Miracles of the Devil" at the Ataneo Popular in Oviedo.

1927 Completes *Novelas selectas de Voltaire,* a translation of selected novels by Voltaire.

1928 Marries Rosalía Martín. Publishes *Novelas selectas de Voltaire.* Completes his first original full-length play, *Otra vez el Diablo* (The Devil again).

1928–1930 Serves as elementary-school superintendent in the Valle de Arán, where he lives in relative isolation.

1929 Finishes writing *La sirena varada* (Mermaid aground). February: premiere, in Zaragoza, of *El crimen de Lord Arturo,* a dramatic version of Oscar Wilde's *The Crime of Lord Arthur of Savile.* Produces an edition, with introduction, of Fray Luis de Leon's poetry.

1930 Publishes a book of poetry, *La flauta del sapo,* the first work to carry his pseudonym, Casona.

1931 Spain becomes a republic. Casona returns to Asturias as a school superintendent in Oviedo. He offers *La sirena varada* to the Xirgu-Borras company; despite Miss Xirgu's personal enthusiasm for the work, they do not present it.

1931–1936 Works for the Republic with the Inspección Provincial de Madrid (Madrid's Provincial Inspection Bureau), leading several cultural missions to Spain's provinces.

1932 Pubishes *Flor de leyendas* (Legendary gems), which garners the Premio Nacional de Literatura.

1933 Enters *La sirena varada* in a contest for the Lope de Vega prize, which he wins.

1934 March 17: triumphant premiere of *La sirena varada,* Teatro Español in Madrid.

1935 January: *El misterio de María Celeste* (The mystery of María Celeste) premieres in Valencia; in July the same play has brief exposure in Madrid. April 26: premiere of *Otra vez el Diablo,* in Madrid's Teatro Español. December: *Nuestra Natacha* (Our Natacha) premieres in Barcelona.

1936 February 6: premiere of *Nuestra Natacha* (Our Natacha), in Madrid's Teatro Victoria. Civil war begins in July.

1937 February: begins exile in France. March: embarks for America as artistic director of the Díaz-Collado theater company. June 12: premiere of *Prohibido suicidarse en primavera* (No suicides in springtime), in Mexico's Teatro Arbeo. December 28: *El crimen de Lord Arturo* is presented in Havana.

1938 Gives many lectures. June 17: premiere of *Romance de Dan y Elsa* (Ballad of Dan and Elsa), Teatro Nacional (Caracas).

1939 May 21: premiere of *Sinfonía inacabada* (Unfinished Symphony), in Mexico's Teatro Solís. June:

Chronology

establishes residence in Buenos Aires and joins "Argentores."

1941 Finishes *Las tres perfectas casadas* (The three perfect wives), which premieres on April 18 in the Teatro Avenida in Buenos Aires.

1944 November 3: premiere of *La dama del alba* (*Lady of the Dawn*), Teatro Avenida (Buenos Aires).

1945 August 24: premiere of *La barca sin pescador* (*Boat Without a Fisherman*), Teatro Liceo (Buenos Aires).

1947 June 19: premiere of *La molinera de Arcos* (The miller's wife), Teatro Argentino (Buenos Aires).

1949 April 1: premiere of *Los árboles mueren de pie* (Trees die standing), Teatro Ateneo (Buenos Aires). Publication of *Retablo Jovial*.

1951 June 1: premiere of *La llave en el desván* (The key in the attic), Teatro Ateneo (Buenos Aires). December: premiere of *¡A Belén, pastores!* (To Bethlehem, shepherds!), in Montevideo's Parque Rodó.

1952 March 14: premiere of *Siete gritos en el mar* (Seven cries at sea), Teatro Politeama (Buenos Aires).

1953 May 29: premiere of *La tercera palabra* (The third word), Teatro Odeón (Buenos Aires).

1955 March 8: premiere of *Corona de amor y muerte* (*Crown of Love and Death*), Teatro Odeón.

1956 Visits Europe again.

1957 April 12: premiere of *La casa de los siete balcones* (The house of the seven gables), Teatro Liceo. January 9: premiere of *Carta de una desconocida* (Letter from a stranger), Teatro Sao Pedro (Porto Alegre).

1961 March 16: premiere of *Tres diamantes y una mujer* (Three diamonds and one woman), Teatro Ateneo.

1963 Returns definitively to Spain, establishing residence in Madrid.

1964 October 1: premiere of *El caballero de las espuelas de oro* (The knight with the golden spurs), in Madrid's Bellas Artes theater.

1965 October 12: premiere of *La Celestina,* Casona's version of the classic by Fernando de Rojas, in Madrid's Bellas Artes theater. October 17: Casona dies following open heart surgery.

Chapter One

Alejandro Casona: The Man and His Works

Early in this century, in the impoverished remoteness of an Asturian village, the parish priest recorded, "In the parish Church of San Martín in Besullo, Council of Cangas de Tineo, diocese and province of Oviedo, on March 25, 1903, I, the undersigned, its parish priest, solemnly baptized a child, born the twenty-third of this month, to whom they gave the name Alejandro; he is the legitimate son of Don Gabino Rodríguez y Alvarez and Doña Faustina Alvarez y García. . . ."[1]

The infant, Alejandro Rodríguez Alvarez, would later bring a substantial measure of fame to the little village of herdsmen and artisans, but under a pseudonym, Alejandro Casona, the name he used throughout his professional career. His explanation of his choice of this pen name hints at his love for the village of his birth, a love he expresses explicitly on other occasions.

I was born and reared in an old manorial house which, since it is the largest in the village, everyone calls "la Casona."[2] It is customary in those remote villages (where almost everyone is related and surnames are often repeated) to distinguish families by the place where they live; thus they refer to "the ones from the fountain," "the ones from the Valley," and in my case, "the ones from the Mansion (Casona)." Upon the publication of my first book for the general public, I decided to adopt 'that pseudonym, which I have used from then on. It has come to replace my surname, even in private life.[3]

His affection for Besullo and Asturias is one of the constants in the thematic warp of his theater.

The profession of Casona's parents exercised another influence upon his spirit. They were both teachers, and typically, their profession gave them satisfaction, but not abundance. Alejandro's father had an income of 725 pesetas annually at the time of Alejandro's birth. As is often the case, the drive to improve status and income forced Don Gabino into a life of mobility. An appointment as director of a school in Oviedo led to the first move and to better circumstances. Casona's elementary education, initiated in Besullo, continued in Luarca, Miranda (Avilés), Villaviciosa, and Gijón, all towns in Asturias. Casona's nomadic youth caused no injury to his intellectual preparation. César Tiempo would later describe him as possessed of "one of the most powerful intelligences in Spain."[4] His eager mind absorbed what it could, not only from his studies, but from considerable time spent enjoying outdoor activities. He would later say of his childhood that his clearest memories involved time with the region's herdsmen.

. . . I had a herdsman's childhood. In my book of poems, *La flauta del sapo* [The toad's flute], there are evocations of those days. . . . Yes; to go to the country with the cow herd was my delight. To go with the old herdsmen. I remember one . . . I'll never forget him, if I live a hundred years. That old herdsman told me the most wonderful stories. . . . He knew ancient ballads that enchanted our hours of solitude as we sat with a goad in our hands while the cows grazed in the peace of the mountain.[5]

From his comments, it is easy to trace the beginnings of Casona's persistent interest in traditional materials. He repeats his conviction that there is poetic power in such sources, as is evinced in an interview with Eduardo Zamacois in Buenos Aires, around 1952:

The most durable works will always be the ones most firmly rooted in enigma: . . . panoramas, legends, superstitions, characters from one's native soil. I am certain that just as soon as I set about to formulate a plot, patterns and places from the land where my gaze first fell on the wonder of light begin to awaken in my subconscious mind—that rainy and misty Asturias that in the reminiscence of my childhood smells of forest and moist pastures, the Asturias of mines and sea, of hulking, pick-hewn escarpments and inaccessible mountain tops lost in the gray mystery of the fog.[6]

So marked by tradition are his plays that in the final years of his life the proponents of social theater, the intransigent *engagés*, categorically reject them. We shall have occasion to return to the traditional aspect of his works later.

Formative Years

In Gijón, in 1913, Casona began the studies leading to the *bachillerato* ("baccalaureate") that he would finish in Murcia in 1919 (Shoemaker lists the year as 1917). He also spent a year at the Instituto in Palencia. While still in Gijón, and still very young, Casona read what he considered his first "serious" work, *La vida es sueño* (*Life is a Dream*), by Pedro Calderón de la Barca. Also during that period, he witnessed the presentation of a play, and later wrote of the effect this new experience had on him:

. . . I saw theater for the first time. And it disquieted me terribly, so much that I could not sleep. I had discovered something sensational, a marvelous world. . . . That presentation seemed better to me than any book of stories, better than any novel, better than anything I had seen up to that moment. I had not been able even to dream the discovery of the theater.[7]

It may seem strange that an event remembered with such poignance should remain a bit hazy in certain details—like the name of the play that occasioned such excitement. A footnote by Sainz de Robles in his prologue to the sixth edition of Casona's *Obras completas* (Complete works) reads: "Since I could find no reference to which play Casona had seen on that occasion, Alejandro himself told me that it was *La loca de la casa* by Don Benito Pérez Galdós."[8] Yet José Plans quotes Casona as follows: ". . . I saw my first play. Anita Adamuz presented it in the Jovellanos Theater and its title was *Canción de cuna*, . . . by Martínez Sierra."[9] But perhaps the precise title of the play is not important.

These were obviously impressionable and significant years for young Alejandro. During this time in Murcia, he made his first fledgling forays into writing and acting—which he so enjoyed that he occasionally forgot his school work, and even failed a course in literature! But failure never became a habit with him. Certain teachers encouraged and helped to shape his proclivities as a writer, among them the regional poet Pedro Jara Carrillo, director of the Conservatorio de Declamación at the University of Murcia. Casona collaborated in the publication of several magazines, including *Renovación, Politeknicum,* and *El Liberal,* entered public poetry contests that awarded him diplomas and other prizes, and took part in several theatrical presentations organized at the Conservatorio. Little wonder that he praises so lavishly those years at Murcia:

My years in Murcia (perhaps embellished by distance) are among the best of my life. And naturally, so are the companions of those days that you recall to me: Pepe the confectioner, Pellicer, Antonio Martínez, Prior; and the old teachers, gone now: Andrés Sobejano, Dionisio Serra and the great poet Jara Carrillo. All of them, and all of you, each one a little, have been to blame for my taking this road, the road of the theater—a road that I first took then and have since followed fervently through the length and breadth of so many countries that by now the theater is not what you would call a second life, but my only life. My youth and all its initiations link me with Murcia; and an unbreakable, grateful friendship, and this sort of literary complicity, links me with all of you. . . .[10]

During these colorful years, Casona's affection for the theater got him into minor trouble more than once. Rodríguez Richart suggests that his artistic tendencies, acquiring strength as the years passed, began to worry his conservative parents. And at one point, their fears that he might turn into an irresponsible artist seemed quite justified. He and a friend ran away to join a theatrical company in search of instant fame. But the experience lasted just a few days—luckily, since the "company" abandoned them and they were without food or funds. Casona recalls:

Once we ran away to San Pedro del Pinatar. We were going to give an "impromptu" performance, as they say in theatrical jargon. I was then about eighteen. Another lad and I played out the part of the hungry comics. We were without food or a place to sleep. Finally it occurred to us to untie a boat and drift out to sea to get some sleep that night. The sea was calm and the rest we got permitted us to recoup enough strength to row back to shore as soon as the sun rose. Of course, in the face of such hazards, my enthusiasm for an actor's career waned considerably.[11]

It was shortly following this experience that Casona took employment as a cabinet maker, becoming highly skilled. He loved the trade so much that, if other circumstances had not intervened, he might well have chosen never to abandon it. Rodríguez Richart suggests that the trade was thrust upon him by his parents, who, worried that the Bohemian temptation of the theater would lead to nothing substantial, wanted to ensure his future as a "person of substance," and that he had little affinity for carpentry. But he himself has said, "I had—and still have—a fondness for working with my hands, and the smell of wood is more enchanting to me than the smell of flowers."[12] Casona's parents' mobility rescued him from the obscurity that surely would have followed had he continued to earn his livelihood as an artisan. They moved to Leon, whence Casona enrolled in the Escuela Superior del Magisterio in Madrid, an institution for the training of primary-school superintendents and normal-school professors.

He studied in Madrid from 1922 to 1926, continuing through those years to turn out poems, among them a poetic tale, *El peregrino de la barba florida* (The pilgrim with the flowing beard), for which Eduardo Marquina, the famous Catalán playwright and poet, wrote a flattering prologue. Nevertheless, Casona later disowned it. The title itself recalls Rubén Darío's *Portico,* which refers to Hugo as "the emperor with the flowing beard," and also to Darío's model, Victor Hugo's *Aymerillot,* which speaks of "Charlemagne, empereur à la barbe fleuri" ("Charlemagne, emperor with the flowing beard").[13] One of José Plans's interviews with Casona clarifies the latter's motives for rejecting *El peregrino de la barba florida:*

My first poems, as is always the case, were not really "mine"; they were resonances and remembrances of things I had read. The poet I most admired when I was twenty was Rubén Darío, whom I continue to admire but in a different way. When I discovered Antonio Machado my poetic life changed completely. The simplicity, the naturalness, the assonant rhyme, the words well rounded and smoothed by centuries like a pebble polished by a stream seemed much more human and profound than the violins and Parnassianism of Rubén. So I tore up what I had written and resolved to start over. I destroyed everything I had published. . . . I was not satisfied with that early . . . literary stuttering.[14]

José Balseiro and J. Riis Owre trace what they perceive as an influence on Casona from Ramón del Valle Inclán, partially because of the medieval atmosphere surrounding the pilgrimage to Santiago de Compostela in *El peregrino*. They see this influence persisting, though attenuated, in his first plays.[15]

Young Manhood

In 1926, the "formalities" of his education completed, Casona took a position as a teacher in an elementary school in Madrid. The following year saw him back in Asturias, in Narcianda, near Covadonga. His duties in these posts obviously did not occupy all his time, for in 1926 he completed a translation of Thomas De Quincey's *Confessions of an English Opium Eater* (which he titled *Los placeres y los tormentos del opio*), and in December of that year he gave a lecture on "The Life and Miracles of the Devil," at the Ateneo Popular in Oviedo, a topic based on the thesis he wrote at the Escuela Superior del Magisterio. The title of his thesis was *El diablo en la literatura y el arte* (The devil in art and literature). This was the first of many public lectures that he would give during his productive lifetime. In 1927, he completed *Novelas selectas de Voltaire,* which, besides the translation of "selected novels" of Voltaire, contains a perceptive introduction to Voltaire and his works.

The year 1928 proved equally eventful. The *Novelas selectas de Voltaire,* completed the previous year, was published, he received an appointment from the Ministry of Instruction as elementary-school superintendent in the Valle de Arán, high in the Pyrenees, and he married Rosalía Martín, who had been fellow student, sweetheart, and muse to him during his years at the Escuela Superior. And perhaps most important, from the point of view we are considering, he completed his first original, full-length play, *Otra vez el Diablo* (The Devil again), a work reflecting the same interests he had revealed earlier in his thesis.[16] This was the play he submitted in a drama contest sponsored by the *ABC,* a daily newspaper in Madrid. His friends in the capital had read the manuscript before he finished it, and they urged him to write the ending and enter the competition.[17] Thus encouraged, he took advantage of the uneasy period during which the entries were being judged to take a copy of his play to the Josefina Díaz company. Santiago Artigas, Josefina Díaz's first husband, read it and reacted negatively. The play contained too many innovations to offer any box-office security, he said, but added that if it should take first place in the contest they would produce it. So it was discouraging to Casona when he learned that his work had won a prize—third, an honorable mention (which actually speaks rather highly of his early effort).

Casona and his wife were three years in the Valle de Arán, the village of Ses. Those were productive years, though the experience was a bit lonely, almost in the nature of a confinement, as Casona himself expresses it:

I was a country schoolteacher. During Primo de Rivera's dictatorship, they sent me to work in the Valle de Arán. It was almost like being exiled because in the raw cold of northern Spain, the ice flow from the Pyrenees cuts us off from the rest of Spain. There I founded, with the schoolchildren, a children's theater, "El Pájaro Pinto" ["The Speckled Bird"], which operated on the basis of a primitive repertoire, "Comedia del arte," traditional sets, and local dialect. We were successful. The youngest children were entertained and the older ones learned lessons and received instructions that stirred their imaginations and would never be forgotten.[18]

Both Constantino Suárez and José Rodríguez-Richart remark on the great accomplishments of those years in "isolation." Besides his work with the children, Casona translated four one-act plays by August Strindberg; turned out an edition with an introduction of selected poems by Fray Luis de León on the occasion of Fray Luis's centenary; wrote *La sirena varada,* the play destined to launch him as a dramatist; adapted Oscar Wilde's story *The Crime of Lord Arthur of Savile* for the stage (it was presented in Zaragoza by the Ladrón de Guevarra-Rivells Company); and published a book of poetry, *La flauta del sapo* (The toad's flute), which elicited a gratifying reaction from José María Souviron, who called Casona a "rural poet of great lyricism."[19] This latter work he printed on a school press, for which he himself set the type, on paper smuggled in from France. It was the first of his works to carry the pseudonym Casona; all previous works he had signed A. Rodríguez Alvarez.[20]

But this is not all. In addition to these accomplishments, staggering for so short a period, Constantino Suárez affirms that Casona raised the level of public education in that region by establishing dining halls, clothing exchanges, and scholarly libraries, and he donated his time and means in giving complimentary classes and educational materials to the schools.[21] Poet and teacher—these qualities persist in Casona the dramatist throughout his career. Juan José Plans records Casona's thoughts on the teaching profession:

> I feel very deeply the teacher's call. Some critics have reproached me for letting it show through in my theater. I learned to respect the profession through my parents. . . . But it's the most difficult profession I know. To be dedicated to it fully, one needs strength, cheerfulness, faith, fervor, and a very steady hand, because—like the surgeon—it is in his hands, just a millimeter away, to form or destroy the soul of a child. One old teacher said, "When you don't feel capable of running up the stairs two at a time and singing, then get out." So I got out.[22]

Before doing so, however, he continued to function with great energy in his profession. In 1931 he returned to Asturias, where he briefly occupied the post of school superintendent in Oviedo, of little significance for his career, though he did help to found a shortlived republican newspaper called *Víspera*.

During that same year, on April 14, Spain became a republic, with profound effects on Casona's life and career. Through public examination, he won a post with the Inspección Provincial de Madrid,[23] a position he retained until 1936. The new government established the Patronato de Misiones Pedagógicas for the purpose of spreading culture and fomenting appreciation for Spain's artistic heritage among those of the rural areas of Spain. D. Manuel Bartolomé Cossío, disciple of the great educator D. Francisco Giner de los Ríos, received the nod as director of the Patronato and chose Casona to lead in the organization of several projects. Casona headed or participated in eight of the nineteen missions for 1932 and four of twenty-four for 1933,[24] and led a special mission to the impoverished town of San Martín de Castañeda (Zamora) in 1934. But Casona's principal contribution to that bold program came in his appointment as head of the Teatro del Pueblo,[25] a company of some fifty students who donated Sundays and vacations and time stolen from studies to bring a spot of joy to the people in the culturally deprived regions of Spain. Shoemaker has explained the purpose of these missions:

> Briefly stated, the *misiones* sought to perform a work of social justice by bridging the abyss between the cities and the rural districts and by removing through communication the isolation of the latter. Working with or through the *maestro* of each village, the *misiones* supplemented the schools but differed from them by bringing freely to whole communities—men and women and children of all ages—new and stimulating cultural experiences. The visit of a group of *misioneros* would normally last a few (five to ten) days and would include the showing of motion picture films, the reading of pieces of good literature (often national poetry), talks on such subjects as personal hygiene and practical agronomy, the playing of fine recorded music, and the performance of short plays. Sometimes a puppet theater and teacher-training courses were included. The *misión* had to provide all its own equipment from electric generator to portable stage. And at its departure, it left behind a small and well selected library, or a phonograph and records, and a desire in the village for a return visit. The school taught how to read, the *misión* awakened the love of reading. By opening the windows of the mind to new vistas of many sorts the *misiones* were bringing hundreds of villages to life, reincorporating them into the Spanish nation.[26]

The troupe presented their first performance on May 15, 1932; their final performance took place in a military hospital during the first few weeks of the Civil War.[27] The performances during that brief period totaled approximately four hundred, in 115 villages of Castilla, La Mancha, Extremadura, León, Aragón, Asturias, and Galicia. Casona never regretted the tremendous expenditure of energy the project required. Writing in 1949, he remarks:

> During the five years that I had the good fortune to direct that student group, more than three hundred towns . . . watched us come to their plazas or porticos, set up our equipment in the open air and present our seasoned repertoire before the happy astonishment of the village. If I can pride myself on having done any work of beauty in my life, that was it; if I have learned anything serious about theater and the

common people, I learned it there. To be in charge of three hundred performances by a student cast before an audience of primitive wisdom, emotion and language is an educational experience.[28]

As might be expected, Casona threw himself into the project with total commitment. Of the thirteen titles in the group's repertory, Casona contributed four.[29] Among his contributions, we can list a two-act abridgment of Leandro Fernández de Moratín's *El médico a palos,* a translation of Molière's *Le medecin malgré lui* (*The Doctor in Spite of Himself*). He also wrote three one-act plays on themes well known: *El entremés del mancebo que casó con mujer brava* (Farce of the youth who married a shrew) based on *Enxiemplo XXV* of *El conde Lucanor; Sancho Panza en la ínsula* (Sancho Panza on his island) from part 2 of *Don Quijote;* and *Balada de Atta Trol,* adapted from a work by Heinrich Heine. In addition, Constantino Suárez lists several speeches Casona delivered in connection with the Patronato.[30]

Casona did not neglect his writing, even during those happy but hectic days with the Patronato. Suárez cites the reviews *Estampa, Dos, Agora, Eco,* and *Social* (Havana) as publishers of both prose and verse by Casona.[31] During a summer vacation spent in Canales, his mother's native village, he penned *Flor de leyendas* (Legendary gems), which garnered the Premio Nacional de Literatura ("National Literary Prize"), established by the Ministry of Public Instruction. Critics enthusiastically seconded the judgment of the jury, and Casona's name began to acquire the renown that would later become synonymous with it.

Theatrical Success

As indicated, Casona had completed two original plays, *Otra vez el Diablo* (1928), and *La sirena varada* (1929), offering *La sirena varada* to the Xirgu-Borrás company in 1931, but they had never presented it, notwithstanding Xirgu's apparent personal enthusiasm for the play. So, in 1933, Casona decided to enter the script in a contest for the Lope de Vega prize, sponsored by the Ayuntamiento ("Town Council") of Madrid. The winner would net ten thousand pesetas and the performance of his play in the Teatro Español. With no fewer than 116 competing entries,[32] Casona held little hope of winning, but was pleasantly surprised, as seen in his own account of how he learned the happy news:

The news came to me while I was on board a streetcar. It was 9:00 o'clock at night. I was headed home, and bought a *Madrid Herald.* There was a political crisis at that time and the newspapers carried large headlines. I thumbed through the paper. . . . In it . . . , in the inner pages, I saw the entry: the "Lope de Vega" Prize for *La sirena varada* [Mermaid aground]. [At first] I was bewildered. Then I was seized with an impulse to wave the newspaper and begin shouting, "My play! It's my play! One of mine!" I jumped off the streetcar and stood there in the street without knowing what to do, silent and confused for a long time. Finally, since I didn't know what else to do at the moment, I thought, "Fine! Now why did I get off the streetcar?" I waited for another one, got on and went home to tell my wife.[33]

March 17, 1934, marks the date of the play's premiere. The Xirgu-Borrás company, among the most prestigious in Spain, the same that earlier had long hesitated over presenting the work, staged the production so successfully that the playwright's career was no longer in question. The company took the play on tour to all the major Spanish cities, with successes repeated many times over in subsequent years in South America, the Antilles, New York, Italy (it played in six Italian cities), and Paris. The play had a successful run in Río de Janeiro and Lisbon, with a different Portuguese version in each city, and also has been translated into Polish.

La sirena varada was actually Casona's second play to be professionally presented. The first, as we briefly noted earlier, was his adaptation, *El crimen de Lord Arturo,* presented with tepid success in Zaragoza in 1929. His third attempt resembled the first. *El misterio de María Celeste* (The mystery of María Celeste), the dramatization of a short novel by Hernández Catá, and written in collaboration with the novelist, had its brief, pale day on stage in January 1935, in Valencia. Though it did not die there, since it had another short exposure in July of that same year in Madrid's Teatro de la Zarzuela, the play seemed to give very little satisfaction to Casona, as he did not include it in his complete works, nor has it been published anywhere. Shoemaker records that it was filmed, however, in 1944.

Much more satisfying was the successful mounting of Casona's first original play, *Otra vez el Diablo,* on April 26, 1935, in the Teatro Español. His earlier failure had not dampened his faith in the work, which he had reworded a bit to conform to current stage conventions. The critic for the newspaper *El sol* described it as "a symbolic theater of fantasy, but also educational, moral and imbued with internal values."[34] Others have also noted Casona's didactic penchant in this play.[35] Several Spanish editions have appeared, and it has been translated into French. With its success, coupled with the larger triumph of *La sirena varada,* Casona emerged permanently from anonymity, ready for even greater public acclaim, which arrived with the premiere of *Nuestra Natacha* (Our Natacha) in December 1935 in Barcelona. Its debut in Madrid came two months later (February 6, 1936) in the Teatro Victoria. So resoundingly successful was the play that it achieved a run of five hundred consecutive performances, a triumph unequaled prior to that point in Spain's theatrical history. It may be, as Shoemaker suggests, that political and social tensions of that period favored reception of the play's message, because the press lavished unstinting praise on it. Not one dissenting critic raised even the mildest negative criticism, a fact that may in itself be something of a record for our century. Natacha, the play's heroine, rises above her obscure beginnings to conquer the cruel and obtuse pedagogical conventions that made her own education a nightmare. Her forward-looking and kindly educational programs achieve the rehabilitation of delinquent orphans with whom she identifies, for she herself trod the paths they are forced to tread.

Shoemaker comments on the widespread notoriety that Casona achieved with this play:

News of the play's success spread so fast that it was soon being performed simultaneously by almost all the theatrical companies in Spain and Spanish Morocco, even in the small towns. At Barcelona it was performed in two theaters at the same time, in Castilian in one, in Catalán in the other. The fame of the play soon crossed the ocean and performances were given in most of the theatrical centers in Spanish America. Nearly all the important actors and actresses on both sides of the Atlantic have played Lalo and Natacha, the most prominent being María Fernanda Ladrón de Guevara (Barcelona, 1936), Lola Membrives (Buenos Aires, 1936), Margarita Xirgu (Mexico City, Havana and Bogotá, 1936–37), Alejandro Flores (Santiago de Chile,

1936), Eugenia Zúffoli (Caracas, 1937), and Asunción Casals (Barcelona, 1936; in Catalán). At least fourteen professional companies have done *Nuestra Natacha* on the stage. Four editions in Spanish have already been published. A French translation had a hundred performances in Paris in 1944 and 1945 and then went on tour. The play was done in Czech in Prague in 1936 and in Portuguese in São Paulo, Brazil, in 1943. Three motion picture versions have been made— one each in Spain, in Brazil and in Argentina.[36]

On March 26, 1936, a group of fellow writers and artists honored Casona at a banquet, a gathering that appears to have provoked many Fascist *falangistas* to a fever of vindictiveness. Casona's interpolated criticism in *Nuestra Natacha* of the conservative "señoritos"—"idle and irresponsible sons of wealth and position, . . . who had already flocked to . . . the Falange"[37]— seems mild and unobtrusive by present standards, but it apparently contributed to dreadful reprisals taken later. José Balseiro and J. Riis Owre, suggesting certain parallels between *Nuestra Natacha* and Galdós's *Electra,* remark:

Casona took no part in politics, and it may be that he wrote this play with no militant purpose in mind. Perhaps the same may be said of Galdós. But because of *Electra* the Conservative cabinet of Marcelo Azcárraga fell and was succeeded by the Liberals under Sagasta. When *Nuestra Natacha* opened in León two days before the outbreak of what Casona has called "la hondura total de la tragedia" its author was marked as a republican, and all those who had gathered there at a banquet to celebrate his triumph were later executed.[38]

Exile and Wandering

Later that same year, Casona fled Madrid, taking refuge in Asturias, where he left his wife and daughter with relatives, assuming that they would be out of danger there. He then followed a circuitous route back to Madrid, witnessing the apex of its siege in November. The Fifth Regiment managed finally to evacuate him to Valencia, where he learned that his family in Asturias was in great peril, their village having fallen to the rebels. Not until after he had reached asylum in France, in February 1937, could he be assured of their safety. Though his cousins had been shot, Rosalía and Marta still lived, and he eventually managed to bring them to a small town in the Breton peninsula. Destitute and forced to accept the largesse of friends, he was spared returning to Valencia and the perils of war by a telegram from the theatrical company of Pepita Díaz and Manuel Collado, offering him a position as director. He did not hesitate to accept the offer and, in March 1937, set sail for Mexico, the first of many Latin American countries the Díaz-Collado company would tour. With them, besides Mexico, he eventually visited Cuba, Puerto Rico, Venezuela, Colombia, Peru, Chile, and Argentina, working with the company in varied productions, including many of his own works, and presenting lectures from time to time on a broad range of topics. He finished *Prohibido suicidarse en primavera* (No suicides in springtime) in Mexico, and saw its premiere in the Teatro Arbeo, Mexico City, on June 12, 1937. Margarita Xirgu, sensing the play's potential, took it to successful performances in Buenos Aires in 1937 and Montevideo in 1938. It has since been published in at least four different Spanish editions and translated into Portuguese, Italian, and Dutch.

Cuba followed Mexico in the Díaz-Callado itinerary. There Casona reworked *El crimen de Lord Arturo,* and there the new version appeared in a theater in Havana, on December 28, 1937. Federico Carlos Sainz de Robles ends a rather long encomium of the play with these comments:

No, don't think that I'm going to declare that the magnificent Irishman himself could not have made a better adaptation. Why talk nonsense? It is sufficient to affirm that with the one made by the admirable Spaniard . . . we don't miss the one that the originator of the tale did not make.[39]

In San Juan, Puerto Rico, the company's next stop, Casona again successfully mounted *Prohibido suicidarse en primavera* and finished writing another play, *Romance de Dan y Elsa* (Ballad of Dan and Elsa). It premiered later, on June 17, 1938, in Caracas in that city's Teatro Nacional. The Díaz-Collado company produced it first, but another group, the Mecha Díaz company, added it to their repetoire and presented it in three of South America's major capitals, Buenos Aires, Montevideo, and

Santiago, during 1939 and 1940. It opened in Buenos Aires on September 15, 1939, and had a run of a hundred performances. Yet critics were not enthusiastic. Typical of critical reaction is the opinion of a Buenos Aires reviewer that the work fell far short of the promise shown by plays such as *La sirena varada* and *Nuestra Natacha*.[40]

The year 1938 found Casona back in Mexico for a brief period, during which he wrote the following to José Balseiro:

We'll leave Mexico in a couple of weeks and we'll take the usual theatrical tour along the Pacific coast: Panama, Colombia, Guayaquil, Chile. From June to November we'll be in Buenos Aires (Ateneo Theater). I have a new play there, *Sinfonía inacabada* [Unfinished symphony], which I have finished just recently.[41]

Sinfonía inacabada had its premiere in the Teatro Solís. The Díaz-Collado troupe presented it on May 21, 1940, taking it later to Buenos Aires (1940) and Santiago de Chile (1941). The audiences received it well, critics much less so, showing the same lack of enthusiasm that they showed for *Romance de Dan y Elsa*.

The tour with the Díaz-Collado company ended in 1939. Casona's tight affiliation with that company seems to have expired, for all practical purposes, with the presentation of *Sinfonía inacabada,* though, as Rodríguez Richart affirms, he did renew his collaboration with them from time to time thereafter. His work with the company proved fruitful and rewarding, but his energies also found an outlet in the many lectures he delivered at various cultural institutions, among them the Palacio de Bellas Artes and the Universidad Popular in Mexico City; the Teatro Nacional, the Teatro Comedia, and the Sociedad Hispano Cubana in Havana; the University in San Juan (Puerto Rico); the Ateneo Literario in Caracas; the Teatro Municipal in Santiago de Chile; and several centers in Montevideo, Buenos Aires, La Plata, and Rosario.[42]

Refuge in Argentina

In June 1939 Casona established residence in Buenos Aires, severed his tie with the Society of Spanish Authors (Madrid), and joined Argentores (The Society of Argentine Authors). Among the many activities he engaged in while there, one of the earliest was a play, *María Curie*, which he wrote in collaboration with Francisco Madrid. The effort, as Rodríguez Richart remarks, seems to prove that collaborative endeavors were not favorable to Casona's art or his artistic temperament. Casona did not include the play in the collection of his complete works, nor has it been published elsewhere, though it achieved moderate success when presented.

In Buenos Aires, Casona involved himself in the production of motion pictures and television, which absorbed a great deal of his time. In 1941 *Las tres perfectas casadas* (The three perfect wives) appeared, following which there came a lapse of three years without a new play; however, he did produce during that period no fewer than eight movies, some originals and some adaptations. *Las tres perfectas casadas* occasioned a brief source of bitterness for Casona. A belated and obtuse charge of plagiarism came in 1950 from a reporter for *ABC,* whose homework fell short of professional thoroughness:

At the announcement of the revival of the famous play attributed to Alejandro Casona, *Las tres perfectas casadas,* to be presented by the Anita Lasalle company in the Teatro Liceo, a play that was the great hit of the season a few years ago and has since been presented thousands of times, it was discovered that the work is not original with that author. Casona himself has submitted a document acknowledging that fact to the Society of Authors, in which he declares that he has dramatized a German story. In view of this, a part of the author's royalties should go to the author of the original idea; but in that case, Mr. Casona should also reimburse the original author for all that he earned previously for the part that was not his which he has earned up to now as the author of an original work.[43]

Casona's reply sets the record straight:

In 1941 I wrote and presented [the play] in Buenos Aires. . . . [It was] inspired in its point of departure . . . by the famous story by Arthur Schnitzler, *Der Tod des Junggesellen*. This reference to origin, with all the details of the case, was not "discovered" by anyone, but declared publicly by me prior to the play's debut, as an autocritique, and in a newspaper with no less status and circulation than *La Nación.*

... There was no question, then, of hiding anything, much less such an honorable source of inspiration, although my play was limited to taking only its initial idea from the great Austrian novelist. I developed it [thereafter] along quite different lines, with characters, anecdotes and solutions that were exclusively my responsibility.

In consequence, the moral aspect of the question was intact and perfectly clear from the beginning. The only thing remaining was to settle the economic aspect, that is, the sharing of royalties with the novelist—an impossibility at the time, since all correspondence with Europe was cut off because of the war. When it was over, I finally managed to contact Henry Schnitzler, the son and heir of the writer, exiled in California. I told him of my play and placed at his disposition the pertinent royalties. Mister Schnitzler was kind enough to place complete confidence in me and express his gratitude.

Now that the play is being revived, this private agreement between me and Mr. Schnitzler has been made official before the Society of Authors, as is customary. And that is all. So it may be seen that concealment, indemnity, and fraud have existed only in the imagination of the reporter, whose generous intentions need no comment.[44]

Las tres perfectas casadas opened in the Teatro Avenida in Buenos Aires, April 18, 1941, and achieved a run of two hundred performances, Lola Membrives and her company doing the honors. They then took the play to Montevideo and Santiago. The Mclía-Cibrián company mounted a successful run of one hundred performances in Mexico City. Obviously, the play had enthusiastic audiences, but again, critics were less impressed. While conceding the author's expertise in the structure as a whole and his skill in creating gripping scenes, they complain of the lack of "psychological penetration" into the personality of the principal character, who in this case, unusually, is also the villain.[45]

After the brief hiatus in his writing, while he busied himself with the motion pictures, Casona brought another play to fruition in 1944 with a triumph to equal or surpass that of *La sirena varada*. Early on, critical opinion was favorable, and time has crystallized the consensus that it is one of Casona's best. On November 3, in the Teatro Avenida, Margarita Xirgu opened in the title role of *La dama del alba* (*Lady of the Dawn*), repeating the success achieved in Buenos Aires later in Montevideo (January 1945) and Lima (November 1945). Other companies presented the play in Caracas and Mexico City in 1945. A run of one hundred performances in the latter city provides further indication of how well audiences received the play. Besides the accomplishments already mentioned, the resounding triumph of *La dama del alba* in Spain, when Casona returned years later, together with the successful, widespread circulation of the school edition of the work in this country, the many editions of the work in Spanish (at least six), the translations into Portuguese, French, German, Hebrew, Finnish, Dutch, Greek, Swedish, Czech, and English perhaps explains why many students of Casona regard this as his most outstanding work. José Caso González, for one, considers it "the most mature fruit of Casona's theater," in which "the real and the unreal levels cross and mingle throughout the four acts; and there is no need for anyone to explain the abstractions through elements of fantasy."[46]

Casona's old friends in the Díaz-Collado company launched his next triumph, with the presentation on August 24, 1945, of *La barca sin pescador* (*Boat Without a Fisherman*) in the Liceo Theater in Buenos Aires, where it had a run of two hundred performances. Casona calls the work ". . . a play of fantasy in which the devil appears again, symbolizing the protagonist's conscience, troubled by a crime he did not commit."[47] The theme, attributed falsely to Rousseau but belonging to Chateaubriand, originally concerned a man in Europe who, by secretly willing it, caused the death of a wealthy Chinese mandarin and thus inherited his fortune. Eça de Queiroz treated the theme a little less than a century before Casona did in his novelette *O Mandarim* (1879). Casona's version has had at least four editions in Spanish and has been translated into German, French, Italian, Dutch, Welsh, and English. Most critics smile upon it. The exceptions we will deal with later.

Next, in 1947, came *La molinera de arcos* (The miller's wife), a dramatized version of the folk theme so successfully and delightfully exploited by Pedro A. de Alarcón in *El sombrero de tres picos* (*The Three-Cornered Hat*). Again Casona collaborated with the Díaz-Collado company to effect the play's premiere. They presented it in the Teatro Argentino (Buenos Aires) on June 19, 1947. Measured against the standard of critical praise and successful runs achieved by the two plays preceding it, this one reached only a modicum of success. Translations of the play appear in French, Russian, and Swedish. In Spanish, it has had at least three editions. Federico Carlos Sainz de Robles says of it:

> I do not think that *La molinera de Arcos* is a fundamental work in Casona's theatrical productions, but I do regard it as being propitious for revealing his control of scenic architecture and his genius in selecting from among all the elements put into play to effect a spectacular "sensation" those effects that are definitive and exemplary.[48]

The Pinnacle of Success

Casona delayed two years before launching another play, but it was a play worth waiting for. *Los árboles mueren de pie* (Trees die standing) had its triumphant debut on April 1, 1949, in the Teatro Ateneo (Buenos Aires), Luisa Vehil and Esteban Serrador playing the lead roles. A reviewer for *La Prensa* stated emphatically that this was one of the most satisfying plays that had ever appeared on stage in Buenos Aires,[49] and scores of other critics seconded his enthusiasm. Federico Carlos Sainz de Robles calls this the most universally successful of Casona's plays. A two-year run in Buenos Aires, seven months in Rio de Janeiro, a record of 150 performances in Santiago de Chile, and three months in Lisbon attest to a generally favorable audience reaction to the work. Emma Grammatica, Italy's leading actress, played the lead role before audiences in many Italian cities. It played also in Finland, Yugoslavia, Russia, Poland, Israel, and Germany. In the latter country, it was especially well received. The attraction of the role of the Abuela ("Grandmother") brought the famous actress Elsa Heims out of retirement and her performances added further to her fame. One appreciative reviewer from Stuttgart expressed what many of us have felt:

> It is fortunate that there are in our times other authors beside the existentialists, who see only blackness and desperation in the world in which we have to live, whether we wish to or not. Theirs is one way of looking at the world; the other is that of the Spanish dramatist Casona, who finds in poetry and illusion a remedy for many evils. His *Los árboles mueren de pie* possesses an extraordinary sense of humor, and shows a courageous faith in life without denying the tragic side of it.[50]

Casona gathered other fruits of his labors in 1949. *Retablo Jovial*, five short pieces, including two written years earlier for the Teatro del Pueblo, appeared in print. "Sancho Panza en la ínsula" (Sancho Panza on his island) and "Entremés del mancebo que casó con mujer brava" (Farce of the youth who married a shrew) are the two works in the collection that formed part of the repertory for the Teatro del Pueblo. "Farsa del cornudo apaleado" (Farce of the whipped cuckold) is Casona's dramatic version of one of Boccaccio's tales (Seventh Day, Seventh Tale) from the *Decameron*. "Fablilla del secreto bien guardado" (Tale of the well-kept secret) is his version of an Italian folk tale, and "Farsa y justicia del corregidor" (Farce of the corregidor's justice) is based on Spanish folk tradition. Also, around this time, Casona was able to purchase La Sirena, as he would name it, remembering his first dramatic success. La Sirena was Casona's country home in Punta del Este, Uruguay, where he lived, dreamed, and wrote for many years, looking wistfully toward Spain, a Spain that, as he wrote to José Balseiro, "may never come to me."[51]

With the collaboration of the Vehil-Serrador company, *La llave en la desván* (Key in the attic) opened in Buenos Aires at the Teatro Ateneo, June 1, 1951. An interesting play from many points, it was only moderately successful. Christmas of 1951 saw, among many other things, the renewed collaboration between Casona and the Díaz-Collado company in the production of his delightful seasonal children's play, *¡A Belén, pastores!* (To Bethlehem, shepherds!), presented in the open air in Montevideo's Parque Rodó. It is a play reminiscent of many elements—the pastoral tradition, Spain's old liturgical theater; *juegos de escarnio, pasos,* and *entremeses*.[52] *Villancicos* ("carols") enhance and punctuate the action from time to time, some of them by Lope de Vega, Góngora, Juan Díaz Rengifo, Francisco Ocaña, Francisco de Avila, and Cosme Gómez Tejada de los Reyes.[53]

The Vehil-Serrador company again collaborated with Casona for the mounting of his next play, *Siete gritos en el mar* (Seven cries at sea), which premiered March 14, 1952, in the Teatro Politeama. As often seems to have been the case, critics were cool, the audience warm. Casona was hopeful, as we can see in his letter to José Balseiro dated March 18:

To judge from the ticket sales the past four days it's going to be an event like *Los árboles mueren de pie.* We'll see; it's too soon to take for granted. As yet it's impossible to differentiate between initial curiosity and permanent interest. I'm completely satisfied . . . in this regard.[54]

Casona specifies clearly his didactic intent in this play. "It is evident," says Juan Rodríguez Castellano, "that the main value of this play lies in the psychological study of seven characters and their different behavior when faced with death: 'some bravely, others with resigned impotence, others cowardly, others with feigned arrogance, others in the purification of repentance and pain.'"[55] Charles Leighton points out that Casona's didacticism in this case stems directly from the Spanish baroque theater, a detail unfortunately lost on early critics of the play. Sainz de Robles did not miss the point, however:

Siete gritos en el mar strikes me as the most profound of Casona's theatrical works. It is the one most firmly seated on the border line that separates fantasy and reality. . . . Casona notes timidly that his "impossible play" has an ascending line that reaches up to one of the most original and fertile dramatic forms of the Spanish theater: the *auto sacramental.*[56] But if Casona out of modesty cannot decide to believe it so, I categorically affirm that *Siete gritos en el mar* is a modern interpretation—bold and felicitous—of the *auto sacramental.*[57]

Siete gritos en el mar has had at least four Spanish editions and has been translated into Portuguese, Russian, and Czech.

Further influence from the baroque theater is evident in Casona's next play, *La tercera palabra* (The third word), which first appeared in the Teatro Odeón, Buenos Aires, May 29, 1953. The play's theme repeats to some degree that of Calderón's *La vida es sueño.* Again, classical Spanish antecedents were lost on the early critics, who spoke well of the play but ascribed it to sources Casona himself would not acknowledge. In fact, he seems a little miffed as he complains of his critics in a letter to Sainz de Robles:

The reviewers spoke of Pygmalion, basing their views on the happy coincidence that there is in the play a teacher and an adult pupil;

others timidly suggested the word *Emile* (Rousseau is quoted in the work); and other bolder ones recalled Voltaire's *Candide,* demonstrating at once that they understood nothing about the play and that they had not read *Candide,* since my protagonist comes down from the mountain without having read a single book, while Candide is educated exclusively in the bookish pedantry of Doctor Panglos, and is used to combat firmly the optimistic philosophy of Leibniz. As regards the protagonist's Spanish antecedents, no one saw the ones most evident: the self-taught philosopher of our Arabian from Granada, Aben Tofail; his closest kin, the Andrenio of the first few chapters of *El Criticón* by Gracián; nor his highest dramatic personification in the first act of *La vida es sueño*—also expressly mentioned in the play. By the same token, regarding the title itself, no one noted that the three great words—God, Death, and Love—were joined, not verbally, but expressed in dramatic presence at the final moment, around the armchair where Marga lies in a faint. It does not disturb me that they look for a family background for my characters—I indicate them clearly . . . ; what is unforgivable is to be so openly mistaken about their house, district . . . and even their country.[58]

La tercera palabra has seen editions in translations to the Portuguese, Dutch, German, Russian, and Latvian.

On March 8, 1955, the Teatro Odeón once again supplied the locus for one of Casona's productions, a play that originally carried the title *Inés de Castro.* The Elina Colomar–Carlos Cores company did the honors. Casona lists this play as "version forty-five" of the dramatic history of Inés de Castro. The reviewers, perhaps predictably, spent the bulk of their commentaries on comparisons of Casona's work with preceding versions. One noted that all versions of the story had taken liberties with Fernando López's historical account and Casona's was no exception. His chief contribution, said the reviewer, was in his ability to "modernize" the characters and their language. Casona responded to certain criticisms when he prepared the text of the play for printing under its new title, *Corona de amor y muerte* (*Crown of Love and Death*), adding a brief note that explained his intent in writing yet another version of this legendary heroine's life and death. He says that he hoped to "draw from the gentle shadow of Inés one last secret," which he feels he has found in her "will for martyrdom" and in the dual nature—sensual and mystic—of her love. In his concluding remarks, there is once again a hint of annoyance with those who failed to grasp his intent: "To express this centuries-old reply in a modern voice was a lofty temptation. If I have failed, may this version stand at least as another token jewel in the great Ignesian Crown."[59] *Corona de amor y muerte* has been translated into German, Portuguese, and English.

The famous actress, Luisa Vehil, was engaged to create the leading role in Casona's next play, *La casa de los siete balcones* (The house of the seven gables), produced in the Teatro Liceo, Buenos Aires, on April 12, 1957. Miss Vehil consented to an interview by a reporter for *La Nación,* published on the morning of April 12, in which she expresses her enthusiasm for the role she would play and spoke of the ambivalence of Genoveva's personality, which enveloped the character in a poetic atmosphere. She added that she was no longer moved by the character, because Genoveva had become so much a part of the actress herself that she could no longer consider her plight as she would that of another, separate person. It was as though Genoveva had become another form of her own being.[60] Notwithstanding Miss Vehil's enthusiasm, on the following day a reviewer for the same paper lamented the faulty structure of the play, but mitigated his lament by praising the fluidity of the dialogue and the brilliance of its poetic imagery, which he felt compensated somewhat for the structure.[61]

Earlier that same year, on January 9, 1957, Berta Singerman took on the taxing performance of Casona's *Carta de una desconocida* (Letter from a stranger), a dramatic monologue based on Stefan Zweig's short novel of the same name. It took place in Porto Alegre in the Teatro Sao Pedro. Praising Casona's originality in this single-act play, Sainz de Robles affirms that the playwright was able to say everything the novelist had said, yet managed to add something to Zweig's effort, or at least make concrete certain emotions that a reading of Zweig's novel could only suggest.[62] In the next season, Casona himself directed his modernized version of Lope de Vega's *El anzuelo de Fenisa,* presented in 1958 on May 31, by Luisa Vehil's company in Buenos Aires's Teatro Liceo. Critics praised him generally for this effort. Also during this time, *Tres diamantes y una mujer* (Three diamonds and one woman), a play Casona wrote prior to 1959,[63] had its premiere performance in the Ateneo in Buenos

Aires on March 16, 1961. Reviews were tepid, and although the play sparkles with characteristic humor and engaging personalities, it has not come through as one of Casona's best.

Casona's years in South America reflect the same intense concern for cultural and intellectual involvement that he had earlier evinced in Spain. He has published a variety of articles and essays, over fifty of them, many of which will be useful later in the analysis of his theater. Lectures such as the one he contributed to the memorial series celebrating the centennial of Benito Pérez Galdós, entitled "Galdós y el romanticismo" (Galdós and romanticism), and the one he delivered at the Ateneo Pi y Margall in Buenos Aires (1945), give some indication of the level of his concern. Active also in the motion-picture industry, radio, and television, Casona collaborated in launching some twenty motion pictures, many of them based on his own works. He composed the libretto for the opera *Don Rodrigo*, with music by the famous Argentine composer Alberto Ginastero. The opera had its world premiere on July 24, 1964, in the Teatro Colón, Buenos Aires. Its New York premiere took place on February 22, 1966, in the New York State Theater, Lincoln Center, and later it was staged in the famous Metropolitan Opera House.

Casona's involvement in foreign literature further illustrates the multiplicity of interests he held. Charles Leighton synthesizes Casona's achievements in this area:

> In 1942 he translated Ferenc Körmendi's novel, *A Budapesti kaland* and in 1944 he published a translation, *El Kalévala*, of the national epic of Finland. In 1955 he brought out a new edition of *Flor de Leyendas* with an additional legend hitherto unedited: *Villancico y pasión*. In the field of dramatic literature he has translated (1943) three of Lenormand's plays, *Los fracasados, La loca del cielo,* and *La inocente*, all of which have been staged either professionally or by university groups. In 1952 he translated and had produced *Sombra querida* (Beloved shadow), a version of Jacques Deval's play *Ombre chère*.[64]

Return to Spain

Casona long resisted returning to Spain. In fact, as long as Franco's regime was still in power it did not seem likely that he would ever return. But transcending his personal aversions to that regime were his ties with his homeland, and the yearning to find himself once more on Spanish soil grew obsessively each day. While traveling in Europe in 1956, he stopped over in Barcelona, spending time with his brothers and sisters and his aged father. In 1961 he spent a few weeks in Madrid, then the following year he returned again briefly to be present when, at long last, another of his plays—*La dama del alba*—could have its premiere in Madrid. When the unqualified success of this play was duplicated and perhaps even surpassed by the triumph of *La barca sin pescador,* Casona's resistance completely crumbled. He moved back to Spain in 1963, and Spain came out to meet him. The plays that had made him famous in Latin America and subsequently all over the world made him, temporarily at least, perhaps the most popular playwright in Spain.[65]

Among the successes Casona reaped in his homeland while yet he lived was a play that had its first performance in Spain, a work on which he had lavished a great deal of time and thought. He finally finished it in 1963. On October 1, 1964, *El caballero de las espuelas de oro* (The knight with the golden spurs) had its premiere in Madrid's Bellas Artes Theater, then went on to other cities. The total performances for the play exceeded five hundred in Spain alone. Reviews generally were favorable. Enrique Llovet, quite typically, complains that his impressions of the play were intellectual, not emotional, and that he expected much more "warmth" from a play by Casona. But he lauds the author's technique, his poetic language, and the overall grandeur of his undertaking, and concludes by noting that the audience received the play with enthusiasm.[66] Encouraged by the reception given his plays in Madrid, Casona decided to become his own manager. Where Benavente, a generation earlier, had failed, Casona succeeded admirably. Before he died, he had personally directed all his own plays presented in Madrid except *El caballero de las espuelas de oro, La sirena varada, Las tres perfectas casadas,* and *La Celestina.*[67]

Casona's death came as a result of complications following open-heart surgery. His last day was October 17, 1965. Balseiro and Suárez-Rivero sum up his passing:

Already famous, after twenty-seven years of self-imposed exile, he returned to his country with the intention of finishing two plays, *El caballero de las espuelas de oro* and *La Celestina,* which had been for a long time in his mind and in his heart and which were to count among his most resounding successes. He had also come home to die. Madrid, city of Lope and Quevedo, trembled under the impact of the tragic news when his death was announced and the nation, as well as the rest of the Spanish-speaking world, mourned him.[68]

La Celestina, Casona's adaptation of the famous novel by Fernando de Rojas, was presented almost simultaneously in the Bellas Artes Theater, October 12, 1965. The play triumphed, adding still another success to the long list of excellent achievements by Alejandro Casona, playwright.

Chapter Two
Tradition's Legacy

Casona's statement, "I believe more in men than in books,"[1] shows his preoccupation for the human, the spiritual side of man. Earlier, in his "Preliminary Note" to *Retablo Jovial,* he exulted in his experience as director of the Teatro del Pueblo: "If I can pride myself on having done any work of beauty in my life, that was it; if I have learned anything serious about theater and the common people, I learned it there." Significantly, he joins the words "common people" and "theater" (*pueblo* and *teatro*) and, in a similar vein, praises Antonio Machado's instinct for tradition: "No one has sensed like Machado the supreme artistic value of the things that emanate from the common people or have the power to return to them. With Mairena as his mouthpiece, he once said, with finality, 'in our literature, everything that is not folklore is pedantry.' "[2]

Most of Casona's works betray his idealistic affinity for Spain's common man with his warmth and basic honesty. Charles Leighton has called attention to the tendency to set his plays in rural areas, to allow the action to unfold away from the devious, dehumanized urban centers.[3] *Flor de leyendas,* which won for Casona the National Prize for Literature in 1933, is a sensitively written collection of folk legends from many parts of the world. His *Retablo jovial* contains playlets that reconstruct with admirable dramatic insight Sancho Panza's day as judge in the "Isla Barataria"; one of the tales from *El conde Lucanor* and another from the Decameron; and two popular fables. Critics have emphasized Casona's blend of legend and history in *Corona de amor y muerte,* a play with which we shall deal in detail in a later chapter. Federico Carlos Sainz de Robles points out his tendency toward Calderonian allegory.[4] In short, we must conclude that tradition and history represent a substantial pattern in the fabric of Casona's theater.

In this chapter we shall trace Casona's method of dealing

with legendary material, as well as death and the devil, and especially the folk tale popularized by Pedro A. de Alarcón, "'The Corregidor and the Miller's Wife,' or 'The Miller and the Corregidor's Wife,' " to which Alarcón gives the "more transcendental and philosophic title (for the seriousness of these times requires it) of *The Three-Cornered Hat.*"[5] Casona, confessing that his primary impetus for writing this play was supplied by Alarcón's novelette, gives us some notion of the long-standing popular appeal this theme has had:

> We are facing no unpublished matter here. Nor was Alarcón when he took it up to embroider upon the coarse, primitive burlap [of that traditional tale] the most colorful and delightful of his costumbrista narratives. The traditional account of the Miller's wife and the Corregidor, in a hundred different forms . . . , has gone from person to person throughout the limits of Spain since the beginning of the nineteenth century, until it has evolved from its elemental, primitive form to the loftiest artistic elaborations of the novel and the theater.[6]

La molinera de Arcos (The miller's wife)

Casona's dramatization of the folk tale is set in the early part of the nineteenth century. The title we shall give it is The miller's wife. First, the story

Tío Lucas, the miller, regularly entertains the principal gentlemen of the town. There are many reasons why they gather at the humble miller's place, but most important is the miller's wife, Frasquita, a lovely creature devoted to her rough-hewn husband. All the men are content to admire her from a distance except the ranking aristocrat, the Corregidor, who is bent upon a conquest. At the suggestion of his aide, the Bailiff, whose name is Weasel (Garduña)—so named because his qualities are so admirably represented by the animal of the same name— he goes to the mill at the *siesta* hour, knowing that Lucas will be sleeping. Frasquita handles him deftly, however, and his amorous intentions are thwarted. But Garduña has another plan: get Lucas out of the house. It happens that the mill lies within the jurisdiction of a neighboring township, and the mayor of that township would be most willing to do the Corregidor a favor. So Weasel and the Corregidor arrange with the mayor to have Lucas arrested and jailed for a night, with plans to dismiss the matter as a mistake the following day. The Corregidor, then, shows up at the mill as soon as Lucas has left. But in attempting to assail the wife's window to gain access to her quarters, he falls into the mill-race. Frasquita, hearing the commotion and fearing that it is Lucas who has fallen, unbars the door to see what has happened. Garduña and the Corregidor quickly take advantage of this situation and enter her house. The Corregidor then makes his move, and offers in exchange for Frasquita's affection a choice government position for her nephew. Frasquita, of course, will hear none of it, and orders them out at gunpoint. Thereupon the Corregidor faints, and Garduña, fearing that his master is dying, persuades Frasquita to allow him to put the old lecher in her bed to recover. She leaves in search of Lucas. Garduña, having put His Honor to bed, also leaves.

But Lucas, in the meantime, persuades his captor, Toñuelo, that he must return, for he has chanced to see Garduña slithering toward the mill. When he arrives, he finds the door unbarred, sees the Corregidor's clothes hanging near the fireplace, and notices the paper with the official appointment of Frasquita's nephew on the table. He can only conclude the worst. He soon devises his plan for revenge, however. Donning the Corregidor's clothes, he leaves, muttering, "The Corregidora [governor's wife] is also comely."

But Lucas is no more successful with his lascivious intentions than was the Corregidor, and, following a series of delightful predicaments, everything is made clear: Frasquita has not dishonored her husband, Lucas has not violated the Corregidor's wife. The Corregidor, exposed, is exiled from his wife's bedroom while Lucas and Frasquita return to their domestic paradise.

In a sense, the author who chooses to revive a well-accepted theme skirts certain problems that a completely original theme (which, says Casona, does not exist) might bring. Casona knew before he began to write that the story already had an audience; Alarcón's novelette is one of the most popular of the nineteenth century. So Casona's problem was the *dramatization* of the material in a way that would not only do justice to Alarcón's efforts but merit a few accolades of its own. Clearly, the author's summary is out of the question in the theater. Alarcón has it relatively easy. He simply tells his readers what the miller is like, outside and inside, and likewise summarizes for us the characteristics of Frasquita, Garduña, and the Corregidor. Casona must make his characters do all this for him.

In the first scene, largely expository, the opinions of the women visiting the Corregidora (the wives of the Corregidor's friends) reflect the town gossip about Frasquita. Another picture is disclosed later when we meet Frasquita, who has been invited to the Corregidora's house. The Corregidora, a noble lady in every legitimate sense of the word, is curious to see what sort of person Frasquita is, and to learn whether her role in the Corregidor's infatuation is innocent or malicious. Before Frasquita's arrival, the other women (the Corregidora, the Fiscala, and the Comandanta) have come together to discuss their respective husbands' frequent absences from home. Present also is Ama, the housekeeper and principal authority in the Corregidor's household. The women, knowing that their husbands are spending their time at the mill, grope for reasons to excuse them. Perhaps they go to drink; . . . the miller serves a delicious wine that makes the blood tingle. Ama, with unswerving frankness, points out that what is in the mill is a woman (Frasquita) ". . . who can cause more sighs than the morning star." The Comandanta[7] and the Fiscala are scandalized to a point just short of apoplexy, as is evident in the following brief portion of this scene:

> *Corregidora.*—Be calm, ladies, be calm. And you, Ama, be quiet! . . . Let's think this out carefully. Before entering the battle, the first step is to study the enemy. Does one of you know the miller's wife?
>
> *Comandanta.*—By sight. A mountain girl from Navarra who arrived in sandals and now wears shoes of fine morocco leather. She's more clever than her station requires and more pretentious than her husband should allow. Grist for the scandal mill.
>
> *Fiscala.*—A temptress! One only needs to see her cross the square on festive days in her twilled blouse and her tasseled mantilla, with that air of independence and those bare arms, looking at the men as though challenging them.

Corregidora.—Comely?
Commandanta.—Showy.
Fiscala.—So so. Actually, one never really knows what men are looking for. What has that woman got that we haven't got?
Ama.—As far as *having* it is concerned, she probably has the same things. It's a matter of proportion . . .

Frasquita is characterized as a hussy by the Corregidora's two friends. Ironically, we are disposed to see her otherwise, for we acquire an early antipathy for these euphuistic fugitives from *Les Précieuses ridicules.* Frasquita's appearance corroborates this disposition. After they exchange the customary polite greetings, the Corregidora and Frasquita broach a variety of topics. The Corregidora tells Frasquita that she has heard many flattering things about her. Still, there are details that make one wonder a little. "I know," says Frasquita. "They say that I come and go alone, that my arms are uncovered, that my disposition is gay and free, am I right? Well, I come and go alone because to do good I need no guardian; my arms are bare because I work with them; and my disposition is gay because, since I have plenty to eat and a good husband, I get up with a light heart and I go to bed with thanksgiving."

This self-analysis is a mere summary in Alarcón's novelette: "Mistress Frasquita . . . remained markedly different from the countrywomen of the district. She dressed with greater simplicity, freedom and elegance than they, washed herself more frequently, and allowed the sun and air to caress her naked arms and throat." Likewise, Alarcón summarizes the reasons Lucas can afford to entertain his illustrious guests:

"Was the Miller, then, so wealthy?" you will interrupt me to exclaim, "or was it that his distinguished visitors so far forgot themselves?"

Neither the one nor the other. The Miller had no more than a competence and the gentlemen were the personification of delicacy and proper pride. But in times in which men paid upwards of fifty different contributions to Church and State, a fellow as knowing as our Miller found it well worth his while to keep a hold on the good will of the Aldermen, Canons, Friars, Clerks, and the other folk who could pull wires. And so it was said by not a few that Miller Lucas (for such was our Miller's name), by giving a kindly welcome to all and sundry, was able to put by a very tidy sum at the end of the year.

"Your Worship will let me have the old door from that house you have pulled down," he would say to one. "Your Lordship," he would ask of another, "will order them to give me a rebatement on the subsidy, the excise, or the civil fruits. . . ."

Our Miller was always finding occasion for little requests of this nature, and the reply was always a generous and impartial "As you wish."

And so you perceive that Miller Lucas was not precisely on the road to ruin.[8]

It is the Corregidora who asks the question, "How can you afford it?" in Casona's play, and it is Frasquita who answers:

> *Corregidora.*—How does one explain it? If so many go, and all to eat and drink, it's ruin for your husband!
>
> *Frasquita.*—Quite the contrary. You can't imagine what a poor man can save by entertaining many rich men. Don't you get it?
>
> *Corregidora.*—Not even slightly.
>
> *Frasquita.*—I'll show you. (She rises and sits next to the Corregidora, confidently) Here, between us women, we'll not deceive each other. Where does the money come from in my house? A garden and a mill, and that's all. On the other hand, how many holes are there for it to leak out? (Counting with her fingers) Tithes, first-fruit offerings, sales tax, contributions, subsidies, duties, civil fruits, fines, bridge tolls, utilities, and that's enough, because I'm out of fingers and I'd have to start on my toes.
>
> *Corregidora.*—I understand less all the time.
>
> *Frasquita.*—Think for a moment. Where does this "bloodletting" come from? From higher up, right? Well, if you've got good friends in the upper ranks, you'll see what a poor man can save at the end of the year with a little salt and pepper. (She slaps the Corregidora's knee and winks) Is it clear now?
>
> *Corregidora.*—(Laughing, she responds by tapping Frasquita with her fan) Yes, now I see!

The greatest difficulty the dramatist experiences, no doubt, is in representing a character's thoughts, while the novelist has the relatively simple task of telling his readers what goes on in his character's mind. Witness the novel's scene wherein Lucas returns to the mill to confront the evidence of his wife's supposed infidelity:

. . . The reality hurt him less than the suspicion. As he himself had said that evening to Mistress Frasquita, from the moment in which he had lost the one faith which was the life of his soul, he began to change into a new man.
Like the Moor of Venice . . . disillusionment slew all his love at a single blow, transforming at once the nature of his spirit and forcing him to look upon the world as a strange land in which he had just arrived. . . .
When he had reached the kitchen he sat down in the middle of the room and covered his face with his hands.
So he remained for a long while, until he was roused from his meditation by a light blow on one foot. It was the blunderbuss which had slipped from his knees and had chosen that way of attracting his attention.
"No! I tell you, no!" murmured Miller Lucas, face to face with the weapon. "You are not what I want. Everyone would pity *them*, and they'd hang *me*. We are dealing with a Corregidor, and in Spain it is still an unforgivable sin to kill a Corregidor. They would say that I killed him from unfounded jealousy and then undressed him and put him in my bed. They would say too, that I killed my wife simply on suspicion . . . and they'd hang me. Most certainly they'd hang me! Besides, I should have shown myself very small-souled, very little-witted, if in the ending of ·my life I had earned nothing but pity. Everyone would laugh at me. They would say that my ill-luck was very natural, when I was a hunchback and Frasquita so beautiful. No! Nothing of the sort! What I want is to revenge myself, and, after that, to triumph, scorn, laugh, laugh hugely, laugh at everybody, so that no one will ever be able to make fun of this hump which I have made almost enviable, and which would look so grotesque on a gallows."

How can a dramatist represent this scene, legitimately presented by the novelist as a man's thoughts? A century ago, the playwright could have recourse to the aside or the soliloquy; today that convention is clearly passé, and Casona, writing around 1947, was under the greater stricture of modern conventions. He handles the problem simply, but most effectively. Toñuelo, who has arrested Lucas, returns with him to the mill. Many of the questions and caveats Lucas posed for himself in the novel are voiced now by Tony:

> *Lucas.*—... A curse on my blood! (He leaps to take down the shotgun. Toñuelo struggles with him, finally wrenching the firearm from his grasp.)
> *Toñuelo.*—Think for a minute! You'll ruin yourself.
> *Lucas.*—These are things you don't think about. Let go!
> *Toñuelo.*—No! You listen to me first! . . . What are you going to gain by killing them?
> *Lucas.*—My honor as a man demands it!
> *Toñuelo.*—We poor people don't have any honor, Lucas. But a Corregidor! Do you know what they do to someone who kills a Corregidor?
> *Lucas.*—What do I care? I've lost her . . .
> *Toñuelo.*—They wouldn't believe you. They'd say you killed him to rob him, then put him in your bed for an excuse. And dead in the arms of a woman? They'd write love ballads to them and jeering jingles to you. Think about that, carefully, and then if you still want the shotgun, it's up to you and your conscience. I've done what mine tells me to do. (He lays the firearm on the table. Lucas falls into a chair, shaken by tearless sobs.)

Thus what was originally purely narrative material acquires dramatic life.

The delightful subject of the humor in this story could fill volumes. We shall have to be content with a superficial view of what Casona does in this area. The mainspring of humor in this play is what Henri Bergson calls "inversion." "We laugh at the prisoner at the bar lecturing the magistrate; at the child presuming to teach his parents; in a word at everything that comes under the heading of 'topsyturvydom.' "[9] There is double the reason for laughter in the case of the Corregidor, because not only does he fall into his own trap, but all the discomfort he suffers is deserved. There is inevitably a sense of pleasure over justice being done if the one humiliated merits in our minds the debasement he suffers. Vanity has traditionally been the butt of humorous thrusts; society, it seems, cannot abide persistent self-gratulation, and laughter is the corrective with which it balances this excess. The treatment accorded the Corregidor mirrors the democratic Spanish spirit, for he exaggerates the dignity of his position, assuming that he, the one entrusted with upholding the law, is *above* the law. He assumes that the public was made for his profession, not his profession for the public—an "inversion" of common sense. His wife, on the other hand, commands our greatest respect, for, while she does not descend to the social level of Frasquita and Lucas, she respects their position and their right to their own privacy. Only vanity, which seeks to excuse the abuse of office, is reprehensible.

The Corregidor's debasement often comes in the form of a predicament of which he, through his bungling, is the cause. On one occasion, he offers Garduña a substantial promotion if he can arrange a meeting with Frasquita—alone. Garduña is about to rush out the door to accomplish this charge when Frasquita herself appears. Both Garduña and the Corregidor are stunned. The latter is quick to jump to a conclusion. He hastily hides the elaborate necklace he had intended to give her and exclaims: "Frasquita! You in my house! Have you taken leave of your senses? Can you imagine what my wife might think if she finds you here?" Frasquita innocently informs him that it was the Corregidora herself who invited her to come, and the Corregidora, who has no doubt witnessed these proceedings, enters and confirms what Frasquita has said. Garduña and his master find it extremely difficult to maintain a certain dignity as they beat their retreat.

Federico Carlos Sainz de Robles points out that the popular antecedents to Casona's and Alarcón's works "looked more toward knavery and Boccaccian maliciousness than toward verisimilitude."[10] Humor typical of the early fables finds its way into Alarcón's novelette, but in a very discrete, modified dosage. Actually, there is just one paragraph of that type:

Once alone in the street, the other Canon (who was wider than he was tall and seemed to roll as he walked) continued slowly toward his house; but, before arriving, he committed a certain offense against a wall, which would in the future become the cause of a police edict, and said at the same time, thinking no doubt of his colleague,

"And you like Mistress Frasquita, too! And the truth is," he added shortly, "as for being shapely,—she *is* shapely."[11]

Casona seems unable to resist this rustic, rather Rabelaisian touch. He alters the context, but the spirit is the same. Frasquita has already explained how Lucas is able to afford to extend his hospitality to his guests. The following illustrates the point:

> *Lucas*.—. . . I'm glad to find you in such a good humor. It happens that I've been wanting to ask you a favor. Two, in fact.
> *Corregidor*.—. . . Ask me, my boy, ask me. Today, I'm in the mood.
> *Lucas*.—The first is for my friend Curro Colindres, who received this paper from the city council with a warning and a fine.
> *Corregidor*.—For what crime?
> *Lucas*.—According to the specifications of the sentence: (reading) "For having committed a humid offense against the wall of the church, you are fined five pesetas." Since when is *that* a crime? And if it were, the church would be to blame for being next door to the tavern.

To overcome certain problems inherent in the dramatic form, Casona has added the Fiscala and the Comandanta to the dramatis personae of his account, balancing their excesses with the rustic wisdom of another character who, while not an addition to the list of characters in Alarcón's novel, assumes far greater importance than Alarcón's passing mention of her as "the person of most weight in the household." The Fiscala and the Comandanta represent the prudishness of the mothers suggested in the following scene from the novel; Ama represents the earthy honesty of the goatherd Rapela.

. . . When the goatherd gave them such good measure, the marriageable girls there assembled turned very red; from which their mothers concluded that the story was a little *free*. Whereupon they, in their turn, came near to turning the goatherd black and blue. But poor Rapela (for such was the goatherd's name) did not mince matters and answered that there was no reason for anyone to be so shocked, since there was nothing in his tale that even nuns and children of four didn't know.

"If you don't believe it, just think a moment," he said. "What do we gather from the story of 'The Corregidor and the Miller's Wife'? That married folk sleep together, and that no husband likes another man to sleep with his wife."

"And that's truth!" said the mothers, hearing the laughter of their daughters.

"The proof that Gaffer Rapela is right," remarked the father of the bridegroom at this point, "is that all here present, great and small, know well enough that tonight, after the dance is over, Johnny and Manolilla are going to sleep for the first time in the fine marriage bed which Aunt Gabriela has just shown to the girls so that they could admire the embroideries of the pillows."

"And, what's more," said the bride's grandfather, "in the book of Doctrine and even in Sermons, they speak to children of all these things of nature, so that they should understand the meaning of the long barrenness of our Lady Saint Anne, the chastity of Joseph, Judith's stratagem, and many other miracles. . . ."

Moreover, Ama is loyal to the Corregidora and protective as a mother toward her child. The Corregidora in turn is a generous and noble lady in every way, which reflects Casona's lofty personal regard for women in general. He has said:

I think that they are the ones that make us or break us—for good or evil. I cannot conceive of Dante without Beatrice nor Petrarch without Laura. From the time of Troy to this day there has been no catastrophe, ruin, or tragedy that did not have a woman at the bottom of it. They inspire in us love, art, and all the high ideals that are customarily generalized with a capital letter.[12]

Hence, no doubt, the reason why the Corregidora, Frasquita, and Ama seem at times to dominate the action and ultimately control the outcome of the play.

Casona's characters also reveal another of his personal attitudes. The Corregidor, while generally reprehensible in his conduct, is nonetheless capable of a certain dignity in the defense of his own honor. Notwithstanding the fact that he has been taken in by Frasquita's tale about Lucas's extreme jealousy and ferocity—"a man so accustomed to blood"—he does not hesitate to face Lucas directly when his honor is threatened. Lucas, still pretending to be the Corregidor, enters to greet Frasquita et al.:

Lucas.—What a pleasant surprise . . . Greetings, Frasquita. Did you come to thank me for naming your nephew to his new position? You needn't have; you already paid me for that favor last night in the mill.

Frasquita.—And you can think that of me? You? . . . You! Justice, mister Corregidor!

Corregidor.—And immediately! These things are settled man to man! (He throws himself resolutely at Lucas . . .)

Lucas's lack of faith in his wife is implicitly censured. Obviously, the Corregidor is not all black nor is Lucas all white. Casona has said:

I make no attempt . . . to incite anyone to open rebellion against traditional ethic norms. I may be a sinner but I'm no proselytizer. All I'm asking is that little bit of charity without which there can be no real justice. Do you know a bad man who is capable of being bad twenty-four hours of every day, without a single minute of generosity, without a sign of tenderness, without a breath of love? Well, there you have poor sin, in the moralists' judgment seat, under the inexorable view of centuries. Don't condemn it without a hearing.[13]

Good drama demands economy, as does good novelistic technique. But as a novelist, Alarcón clearly has a freer hand than Casona. Paradoxically, a scene Alarcón includes in his novel to *dramatize* the gossip of the townspeople is superfluous in Casona's drama. The chapter entitled "¡Arre Burra!" (translated, "Gee Up, Donkey" by Martin Armstrong) shows a peasant couple commenting upon the fact that "the Corregidor is going early today to see Mistress Frasquita." The woman's innuendos, notwithstanding her husband's remonstrance, imply that not everyone regards the situation as totally innocent. Casona cannot disrupt the flow of action for such a scene, though the same information comes through to his audience in scenes with the Corregidora, the Fiscala, and the Comandanta. He must also cut out certain other scenes, with their corresponding characters, to keep place changes to a minimum. The officers in the neighboring township where Lucas is detained do not appear in Casona's play. He concentrates the action into two sites: the mill and the Corregidor's mansion.

Scarcely a detail mentioned in the play does not prefigure something that develops later. In scene 1 of the first act, the Corregidor tells Weasel that he cannot abide anchovies, but confesses in the same breath that he never refuses them when they are offered to him by Frasquita. His deceit is quite effective, for Frasquita later tells the Corregidora that the Corregidor loves anchovies. The scene ends with the Corregidora, in full knowledge of what she is about, ordering Ama to prepare anchovies for supper.

It might seem strange that Lucas is able to persuade Tony, the one sent to arrest him, to return with him to the mill, in direct violation of orders he has received from his superior, but Casona again is careful to show motivation for that action. Though he tries to look "official" as he makes his arrest, Tony is less imbued with his office when Frasquita seizes the shotgun to defend her husband. Tony is obviously not as strong a character as Lucas, and besides he openly values Lucas as a friend. It is no surprise, then, that the strong-willed Lucas should return in spite of Tony's protests.

Scene 4 is loaded with suggestions of something tremendous that is about to happen, creating suspense in an atmosphere of tension. The Corregidora mentions that it is "the Eve of Saint Jude."

>*Ama.*—What can you expect from such a day? On the Eve of Saint Jude things always happen . . . Horrors and mysteries.
>
>*Comandanta.*—That's right. Wasn't it around Saint Jude last year that lightning struck during a wedding?
>
>*Fiscala.*—And three years ago, when Juan Barbero went to the mountain to look for a nanny goat that had gotten lost, and he never returned?
>
>*Ama.*—That's another story. Juan Barbero went to look for a nanny goat and he found her. Now they're living together in Gibraltar.

Superstitions thereby announce the barrage of events that accumulate before the evening is over, and Ama continues to spice the conversation with her frankness. Many other such examples of dramatic motivation and concentration combine with these to show Casona's care and insight as a consummate playwright. In summary, it can be said that the play makes use of many traditional materials besides the basic theme itself. Ama betrays Casona's penchant for the "pueblo" and his desire to "return" to these common folk, especially as she contrasts with the artificial, euphuistic Fiscala and Comandanta. Casona's humor, while universal, exhibits an occasional touch of the telluric. The principal women characters show how highly he regards women in general. The way he deals with the Corregidor reveals his basic tolerance. He integrates all these elements with impeccable dramatic technique.

Otra vez el Diablo (The Devil again)

Among the topics that have beguiled many of the world's greatest writers is one with which Casona was particularly fascinated. The subject he chose for his final paper in the Escuela Superior del Magisterio in 1926 was "The Devil in Literature and Art." Shortly thereafter, he wrote *Otra vez el Diablo* (The Devil again), and in 1945 he returns to the theme in *La barca sin pescador* (*Boat Without a Fisherman*). He again makes sport of the Devil in his children's play, *¡A Belén, pastores!* (To Bethlehem, shepherds!), which appeared in 1951. His essay "Don Juan y el Diablo" was published in 1935.[14]

Casona's interest in the Prince of Darkness constitutes another manifestation of his affinity for folk material, material "with the power to return to the people." The Devil appears in some form in practically all folk legends. Myths evolve to express a people's basic concepts of life, inherent and universal concepts. Archetypal symbols, with a common meaning for virtually all of humanity and thus inclined "to elicit comparable psychological responses,"[15] tend to deal in opposites. As an example, Philip Wheelwright points to the up-down symbol, up representing the idea of achievement, down representing some idea of debasement or failure. The archetypal view of woman, moreover, offers another case in point. The Great Mother, Good Mother, and Earth Mother contrast with the Terrible Mother; the Soul Mate contrasts with the Siren and the *femme fatale.* So with the archetypal hero. If, on the one hand, we can point to a hero who is dedicated to the salvation of the kingdom, on the other we must be able to find some form of villain bent upon its destruction, an antihero opposed to the hero. In the Christian religion, clearly, Christ is the champion and model of all good, Satan the sponsor of all evil, and both seem to be necessary. Giovanni Papini elaborates upon this "law of opposites" in his controversial book *The Devil,* affirming that

the activity of the Devil is . . . an aid to the salvation of souls because only when people are sorely tried and learn how to overcome their temptation, do they become worthy of the prize of beatitude. A diabolic temptation—when it is fought down and not ceded to—contributes to the work of salvation. Without victory over the demon, there is no true merit, there is no final peace. The acts and weapons of Satan are, then, instruments which lead to salvation against his will. With his odious perseverance, Satan peoples his hell, but at the same time he also peoples heaven. Many would not enjoy the glories of eternal light if they had not happily overcome the clouds of the depths.
And this is evident in the blinding magnificence of saintliness itself. Sanctity is evil conquered and cast down; if evil (Satan) did not exist, neither would the saints. Satan has a job to do which is irreplaceable, a providential mission, and in this sense we may affirm that the Devil is by divine will a coadjutor of God. Satan is the adversary but, without the adversary, there would be no battle; without the battle, there would be no victory and glory.[16]

Casona's essay "Yo pecador" (I, a sinner) points up two things: (1) how well he understood the "law of opposition" that Papini presents and (2) his personal preoccupation with human values and tolerance:

If today I allow myself to break a lance in favor of sin, I do not do so exclusively for its aesthetic values—so many and of such a quality that to deal with them would be to take us too far afield—but also because of its social and pedagogical values, and even—paradoxical as it may seem—for its "moral" values—values of struggle, fortification and passion. Can anyone conceive of a history of Heaven without the Devil? To imagine a totally passive and gratuitous saintliness would be to imagine an absurd victory without an enemy. The same would obtain if we did away with cowardice—we would also eliminate automatically all possibility of heroism; the abolition of Lust would mean expelling from their altars hundreds of saints and thousands of virgins. Saint Agustín of Hipona, who in this case unites wisdom and experience, wrote beautifully that to tread one by one upon our sins is to ascend one by one the steps that lead to God. Goethe, from another point of view, affirmed that history is written with sins. And Leonardo noted piously that "lust is the cause of life, gluttony sustains it, fear protects it, and pain sanctifies it."[17]

Papini introduces his thesis quite seriously; Casona presents his lightly. His Devil, by the same token, shows closer kinship to Vélez de Guevara's *Diablo cojuelo* than to Calderón's awesome *Mágico prodigioso* or Mira de Amescua's Demonio in *El esclavo del demonio*. Casona understands well that, if God is love, as the Bible assures us, then the Devil is the negation of love—the "great absolute Negation."

Casona's Devil is not devoid of supernatural powers, but they are not, especially in *Otra vez el Diablo* (The Devil again), as conspicuous as his humanity. Sainz de Robles, writing of the Devil and Death as they appear in Casona's theater, observes: "Death and the Demon attract us . . . not because of their impressive significance, nor the anguish caused by their eternal presence, but precisely because of their attained humanity."[18] This "attained humanity" is evident in a number of ways. In the children's play *¡A Belén, pastores!* (To Bethlehem, shepherds!) Casona captures the spirit of the traditional Catalán *pastorets*, presented during the Christmas season, in which the Devil—the negation of all the Christmas season represents—is outwitted and abused by the shepherds who are journeying to pay homage to the Christ child. In *¡A Belén, pastores!* this pathetic Devil appears with the added spice of the humiliations heaped upon him by his domineering spouse. This rather pitiable figure, modified with wit and elegance, is the same Devil of *Otra vez el Diablo*. Let the story illustrate the point.

The protagonist is called, simply, the Student. On his way to attend a university in Germany, he is detained and amiably relieved of his possessions by an unusual band of thieves. When they have gone, the Devil appears and offers to "teach him to make himself a soul tempered by fire and steel." The student refuses any association with the Devil, so the latter withdraws, momentarily.

Alone again, the Student soon hears the infectious laughter of the Princess, who is coming to the woods in search of romance; accompanying her is the court jester, Cascabel ("Jingle-bell"). The student converses with the Princess, who, upon learning of his encounter with the bandits, shows lively interest in the bandit captain. The Student falls in love with her, and in an attempt to follow her to return the handkerchief she has dropped, is tripped by the jester. He remains on "all fours," helplessly watching her disappear as the Devil reenters, knowing that the Student is ready now to listen to his proposition.

The Devil, incognito, obtains a position in court as the Princess's tutor, replacing the old one, a stuffy pedant, in order to carry forward his plans to "help the Student form a soul." He propagates the superstition that the Devil can be killed only with his own dagger, and the Princess offers her hand to the one who will accomplish this prodigious task. The entire kingdom places the blame for their misery (epidemic, poverty, imminent war) on the Devil, who professes innocence. They also claim that he has bewitched the Princess, for, while she seems to have acquired strange new interests, all of her former delights no longer hold any charm for her. The true direction of her interest reveals itself, however, when the Student, who with the Devil's aid has become the Captain of the bandits, dashes in through her window to return her handkerchief, kisses her, and departs abruptly.

In the White Rooster Inn, where the bandits assemble, the Devil appears once more to the Student and gives him his dagger with the assurance that he will find occasion to use it. While they are conversing, the Princess and Jingle-bell knock on the door. As the Student goes to open it for them, the Devil empties a powder from his ring into the Student's drink, then disappears via the chimney. The Princess, wearing a red bonnet (as she did when she was a child, seeking "fairy-tale emotions in the mountains"), asks the Student to kill the Devil, which he promises to do. But he drinks the potion the Devil has prepared and is immediately seized with a desire to violate the Princess. He resists, however, and has Jingle-bell tie his hands, instructing him to ride to the palace for help. The stage is darkened momentarily, after which a red light illuminates the face of the struggling Student and a white light the innocent sleep of the Princess. As dawn breaks, the King comes with his soldiers to find the Student alone with the Princess, but the Student produces the

Devil's dagger, dripping with blood, to reassure the King that he has killed the Devil and all is well. He has won the hand of the Princess.

The salient quality of Casona's Devil is his "attained humanity." There is natural curiosity in his question to the student, "Really, now, what do you think of me?", and he is piqued at the student's answer:

> *Student.*—Not bad. I pictured you even uglier.
>
> *Devil.*—Uglier! Sure, they probably told you all sorts of rubbish. People have never learned to behave toward their neighbor. Besides, I recognize I've aged a little and put on weight . . . If you had known me in my youth!

He seems harmless enough most of the time. His only reaction to the Student's quip, "When you get the Devil by the tail, don't turn him loose," is, "That's vulgar!" He later speaks of retiring from his difficult profession. Everyone has misunderstood him—even the saints. "Nevertheless, if it hadn't been for me, *they* wouldn't have existed either! How I worked for their sanctity, depriving myself of sleep, tempting them untiringly at odd hours, sometimes until four or five in the morning! . . . They couldn't understand that in the history of Heaven, they provide the capital and I provide the work."

The Devil confesses that he loved once, many years ago, a girl named Margarita (an innovation on the Faustian theme), but she returned only hate. But let him tell his own story: "Margarita! . . . She was at once melancholic and bright, like rain in the afternoon. Oh! Those who don't know how I loved that woman can never understand what happened afterward. She fell in love with a Dr. Faust, a miserable coward, and one night in the garden she told him that she hated me. I heard her myself, I heard it from those dear lips! And I saw them kissing among the roses! . . . What happened after that . . . is not love anymore. It was jealous desperation." He seems almost on the point of falling in love again, this time with the Infantina, but she unwittingly confesses that she, like Margarita, hates him. Here the question arises, does Casona contradict himself in portraying his Devil with the human, even God-like, attribute of love, though he possess it but for an instant? This would indeed appear to be the case; he has made his Devil so human that he can no longer fit the category of the same personage described in his essay "Don Juan y el Diablo": "Finally, the Devil's great tragedy, according to the theologians, does not consist in doing evil, but in the fact that 'he can do no good, even if he wanted,' the same way that Don Juan's tragedy does not reside in the fact that he does not love, but in his *inability* to fall in love. If one or the other could fall in love once, for just an instant, they would automatically cease to be the two Absolute Antagonists, the two great Rebels, the two Negations."[19]

Casona, again typically adept, employs many types of humor, but the ones most prevalent in this play are *inversion*, previously treated in our discussion of *La molinera de Arcos,* and *irony.* One type of "inversion" described by Bergson has particularly clear reflections in *Otra vez el Diablo,* i.e., the "inversion of common sense," which places one's profession above the public whom that profession should serve. A doctor, for example, would insist that doctors are essential in society, so essential that it really would not matter if a patient should die as long as the rules of medicine were followed. Thus the means substitute for the end, and the public becomes the servant of the profession, rather than the profession the servant of the public. The bandit-intellectuals, the Princess's first tutor, and the King all conform to this description. "To express in reputable language," says Bergson, "some disreputable idea, to take some scandalous situation, some low-class calling or disgraceful behavior, and describe them in terms of the utmost 'respectability,' is generally comic."[20] The bandit-intellectuals of *Otra vez el Diablo* maintain that their profession is a boon to society, as is first suggested by the Captain, who reprimands his band for protesting his procedure:

> *Captain.*—What you want to do is excuse your cowardice—I've noticed it for some time now. You want to abandon this heroic life and go back home, back to society. Shameful! Have you forgotten what society is? A pigsty, lads; morality and honesty have ruined it.
> *Clotaldo.*—We agree, Captain; but we thought . . .
> *Captain.*—Not another word. Anyone who isn't up to staying with the band can leave.

The Student similarly contributes to this inverted logic:

> *Student.*—. . .So you're bandits. Who would have thought it! I supposed this kingdom was far more backward.
> *Captain.*—It is, it is. Up to now it has only had penny-ante thieves, with no romanticism or elegance. As you can see, I've tried to give it a European veneer—but it's like sowing salt.
> *Student.*—They haven't responded to your efforts?
> *Captain.*—Bah—Our people have no concept of literature.
> *Clotaldo.*—We're a nation without ideals. No culture, no aesthetics.
> *Captain.*—The common people hate us and the aristocracy would rejoice to see us hang. It's revolting! In any country to the south, an institution like ours would have a state subsidy. But here . . . Just try to take a few ideals to people made up of merchants and illiterates.

A state subsidy for bandits! They substantiate Bergson's pandect perfectly. He maintains that the more questionable an art, science, or occupation is, the more those who practice it are inclined to uphold it as indispensable for society. They regard themselves as invested with a kind of priesthood before whose mysteries all should bow. "Useful professions are meant for the public, but those whose utility is more dubious can only justify their existence by assuming that the public is meant for them."[21]

There is a wealth of similar comedy in one of the scenes between the King and the old Tutor, whom the Devil replaces. The Tutor applies the vocabulary of his profession to everyday situations, while the King regards everything as intended for his personal well-being. Bergson has again pinpointed the humor of the Tutor: the most common device employed by comic writers to make a profession ludicrous, he maintains, is to restrict it to the confines of its own particular jargon. "Judge, doctor and soldier are made to apply the language of law, medicine, and strategy to the everyday affairs of life, as though they had become incapable of talking like ordinary people."[22] In this scene, the Tutor is discussing the Princess's state of health with the King. He has consulted Paracelsus, and has found nothing

Tradition's Legacy 47

of diagnostic significance. The King is not surprised. "You doctors only learn as we sick people teach you," he affirms with kingly authority. On the other hand, pedagogy, says the Tutor. . . . "What does pedagogy say?" asks the King.

> *Tutor.*—Pedagogy and I, my Lord, agree upon this fundamental aphorism: "Natura non facit saltus."
> *King.*—In English, master Tutor! I've told you a hundred times that Latin attacks my kidneys!

But even in English, the Tutor has a remarkable talent for complicating the absurdly simple. He explains the Princess's "sickness":

> *Tutor.*—Between one age and another, there lies a strange and dangerous gap. Women tend to fill it with sighs and yawns. They dream, they don't eat, they cry for no reason, and they vex everybody. That's called love.
> *King.*—(dryly) Love.
> *Tutor.*—In love with love.
> *King.*—In love with love?
> *Tutor.*—Or perhaps in this case, love of love; love of a concrete man. After all, "nihil volitum quin precognitum."
> *King.*—(Terrible, his hands over his kidneys) What? Translate that for me, blackguard!

After a few more circumlocutions, he finally does translate it: "The Princess has probably fixed her gaze upon some man." The King is astounded. "Really? And he no doubt allowed himself to be gazed upon! Some men are so brazen!" Incredible effrontery! Nevertheless, insists the Tutor, the Princess's symptoms are conclusive. She is in love. But the King is dubious: "No, my daughter is incapable of falling in love without my permission." But there is more, says the Tutor. Among many other things, she has lost her former affinity for logic—"A very suspicious measure"—and she has had her servants bring to her garden ". . . those baroque fountains that have angels leaking water from unexpected and unholy places." The King is aghast:

King.—She did that? Damn . . .
Tutor.—The case is serious. Nevertheless, there may be a solution. "Similia similibus curantur."
King.—(Roaring.) Similo . . . *what?*

"A situation is invariably comic when it belongs simultaneously to two altogether independent series of events and is capable of being interpreted in two entirely different meanings at the same time."[23] This premise, "two different meanings at the same time," includes the areas of humor evoked through such equivocal phenomena as irony, understatement and implication, and play on words.

Irony, by definition, is ". . . language having a different meaning from the ostensible one and which will be understood correctly by the initiated."[24] Dramatic irony is merely a *situation* having a different meaning from the ostensible one; it occurs when the spectators are informed or aware of elements in the situation of which one or more of the characters are ignorant, or where a speaker utters "words which have a hidden meaning for the audience of which he himself is unconscious."[25] The Devil's initial greeting as he meets the Student is "God keep you, master Student," a most unexpected salutation considering the source. He later affirms that he is "católico apostólico romano," and crosses himself to prove it.

His engagement at court as the Princess's tutor enables him, as we have said, to make it possible for the Student to enter and steal a kiss from the Infantina. She has been led to believe (by the Devil) that the first kiss is mortal sin, and when the Devil returns she says, "Mister tutor . . . I'm in mortal sin!", to which he answers, "Already? Congratulations, my dear. A mortal sin will shine on your youth like a jewel." Only the Devil would make such an observation—but the Princess is unaware of his identity. He also becomes the victim of his own sham, however, likewise through the Infantina's ignorance:

Princess.—I need to quiet my conscience. Come with me to the oratory.
Devil.—(Nervous) Madame, I . . .
Princess.—Don't leave me again.

> *Devil.*—Leave you, no, certainly not. But I . . . in the oratory . . .
>
> *Princess.*—I beg you, accompany me. Prayer will calm me.
>
> *Devil.*—In that case . . . (he offers his arm) Let's go.

The Devil in the oratory! The Infantina has previously told him, "At your side I feel like I'm next to the father confessor." When the King comes looking for "Mister Mephistopheles," Jingle-bell, who knows his identity, says, "Shh . . . (serious). Mister Mephistopheles is praying."

La barca sin pescador (*Boat Without a Fisherman*)

The curtain opens admitting us to the plush office of the unscrupulous financier, Ricardo Jordán, teetering on the brink of total ruin. His "friends" and business associates abandon him, and he finds himself alone with his bitterness. Suddenly a visitor, wearing a black suit, appears mysteriously. It is the Devil himself, who promises to restore his fortune if he will complete an already fat list of broken commandments, thus to secure his soul for Hell. The only unbroken commandment: "Thou shalt not kill." Ricardo resists, until the Gentleman in Black (Caballero de Negro) promises him that he will not even have to witness the crime. It will take place in another country, in a town far to the north where he has never been. The victim is Peter Anderson, a fisherman, a man he has never seen. All that is necessary, says the Gentleman, is Ricardo's signature on a document. Ricardo signs.

His fortunes return, and with them his erstwhile friends, but strangely, these things seem of little moment, and he is unable to put aside a nagging remorse. Driven by his conscience, he goes to Peter Anderson's village to visit Peter's widow, Estela. She and the Grandmother (Abuela) lodge him in Peter's house. He hopes to persuade Estela to accept help, but her fierce pride will have none of it. Ricardo grows very fond of the village and the rustic life of the fishermen; and of course, he falls in love with Estela.

Eventually, Ricardo learns that Estela suspects her sister Frida's husband, Cristián, an old rival of Peter's, of the latter's murder. Ricardo is on the point of confessing to the deed when

Frida rushes in to beg Estela to come to Cristián, who has suffered what appears to be a mortal accident and is asking for Estela. The two women leave, and Ricardo, puzzled, receives a second visit from the Devil, who acknowledges that it was indeed Cristián who killed Peter. The Devil was interested not in the material fact of the murder, but in its spiritual implications. He can claim Ricardo's soul because of the latter's *will* to kill. But Ricardo redeems the contract by fulfilling it via a similar spiritual maneuver; he points out that he has promised to kill, and he will kill—without blood, by doing away with the old Ricardo Jordán and becoming a new man. The Devil, nonplussed, has no alternative—he returns the contract and departs.

Estela enters having offered Cristián her forgiveness, which has had the double effect of relieving his heavy conscience and assuaging her own bitterness. Ricardo, his fortune now gone with the Gentleman in Black, will stay here with Estela and become a part of this rustic community.

An arresting though not at all surprising aspect of this play is the author's instinct for developing character through the words spoken. Concerning characterization through language, Walter Blair, John Gerber, and Eugene Garber remark: ". . . Authors often imitate the qualities of talk or of the thought processes. . . . Sometimes the constructions are not only lifelike but also characteristic of certain kinds of people for instance, bad grammar for the uneducated man, choppy sentences for the decisive man, fragmentary sentences—never finished—for the indecisive character, orotund and long sentences for the orator."[26] The present analysis will deal briefly with Casona's sense of compactness in the poetic selection of words used to reveal his characters' personalities.

Ricardo, as a financier, perceives things—even following his "conversion"—in terms of numbers. At one point, the Devil suggests that to destroy hundreds of wagonloads of bananas, as Ricardo has done, just to bring up prices, is a sin against hungry children who have no way of obtaining food. Ricardo protests that he cannot be bothered by such sentimentality— the heart is a bad business advisor. So the Devil suggests that they leave sentimentality and talk about numbers, which is Ricardo's strong point. And indeed it is. Even in his more philosophical moments, he often resorts to figures: "One day," he observes, "we learn that a fisherman from a northern village is going to die, and we shrug our shoulders. Another day, we read that thirty thousand men have fallen on a battle-front, and we go on quietly drinking coffee, because those thirty thousand men are for us nothing more than a number." It is significant that he adds, "And it's not that we have hard hearts. No, it's our imagination that is dead."

The first words of the Grandmother express the monotony of life since Peter died, with images springing from Grandmother's world—the world of homemaking: "A tablecloth for lunch, a tablecloth for dinner. When you fold the tablecloth, you turn down the sheets; and when you smooth out the sheets, it's time to go back to the tablecloth." Another oldster, Marko (Tío Marko), a secondary character whom we have not mentioned, acquires a great deal of importance as a foil for the loquacious Grandmother. His limited vocabulary establishes him as a slow, taciturn personality. Casona sets up a humorous conflict of personalities whenever Marko and Grandmother come together.

Ricardo's statement concerning the importance of imagination points toward one of Estela's dominant qualities. Indeed, Casona the poet reveals his own intense imagination most readily in Estela. The simile is an ever-present part of the language of all his characters, but the choicest images are reserved for Estela. When Ricardo comments that everyone in the village seems to have blue eyes, she says, "It's from looking at the sea so much." Describing the sun after the long winter, she says, "It stuns you like a whiplash as it comes down through the pines." Archibald MacLeish's *Ars Poetica* reduces "all the history of grief" to "an empty doorway and a maple leaf." Similarly Estela compresses the devastation of her loneliness in the wake of Peter's death and at the prospect of Ricardo's imminent departure into the expression, "An oar nailed to the door, and sit and wait. That's all."

Casona, who exalted children's fascination for the marvelous and for fantasy in general,[27] and defends imagination as a bastion against the encroaching dehumanization of society, selects a heroine capable of transforming an inveterate sinner into a repentant soul. Appropriately, she is imaginative enough to understand that life is a duty, and that ". . . in the life of one man is the life of all men." Thus her imagination gives her qualities that transcend the limitations of her environment and make her a soul-mate capable of providing spiritual fulfillment for Ricardo.

The Devil in this play, as in *Otra vez el Diablo,* is as much human as he is supernatural. When he fails to capture Ricardo's soul, it is love—a "detail he always overlooks"—that defeats him. Again, this is significant, in view of the fact that "love is of God," hence is a feeling the Devil, God's opposite, cannot know. His discouragement makes him almost pitiable as he explains, "In a profession as difficult as mine, you can imagine that I'm quite accustomed to failure. But there's never been one like this. I came to steal your soul, and I myself placed you, unwittingly, on the road to salvation. It's enough to make one want to retire!"

Joaquín de Entrambasaguas's observation regarding one of Casona's proclivities summarizes what most of his critics have recognized, i.e., his didactic bent. "It is curious," says Entrambasaguas, "that this teacher with the sweeping vocation of a playwright that is Casona . . . maintains throughout his entire dramatic output, rare occasions excepted, an educational spirit . . . , evident . . . through someone who teaches and someone who learns." Sainz de Robles calls this penchant *pedagogía del alma* ("pedagogy of the soul"). In *La barca sin pescador,* Casona does indeed have something to teach about the human soul. The mechanized jungle of Ricardo's world at the opening of the play sets all human values aside. Nothing seems of greater importance to the characters of the first act than the acquisition of wealth and power, and the world of this act is artificial and devilish. The Devil himself tells us as much. When he first meets Ricardo he explains that he has just come from the stock market—where he has *so many* clients.

There is, of course, no peace for Ricardo in this mire of selfishness. He finds it instead in a poor fishing village, where "the little wheat that there is is real; and the hunger, too." There are many delightful scenes that teach us, and Ricardo, the shallowness of his artificial world. Let us consider just one. Marko is curious about Ricardo's profession:

    Marko.—What did you do back in your country?
    Ricardo.—I played stocks.

> *Marko.*—Ah. (short pause) And after playing what did you work at?
> *Ricardo.*—Stocks aren't a game—it's a kind of a market.
> *Marko.*—A market?
> *Ricardo.*—But not like the ones here. You buy and sell things. We buy and sell the *names* of things.
> *Marko.*—I don't understand. How can you buy and sell wheat without wheat?

Ricardo explains the function of the stock market in terms as simple as possible. "Now do you understand?" he asks hopefully. Marko answers with conviction. "Now I do. A couple of years ago another fellow came through here who did the same thing, but he did it with a top hat that pigeons flew out of. What I'd like is for you to explain the trick."

Criticism and Casona's Ideological Context

La barca sin pescador has occasioned no small stir among critics. One critique, signed by J. M. Velloso, appeared in the weekly *El Español* on March 2, 1963, following the play's opening in Madrid's Bellas Artes Theater. The critic affirms a great admiration for Casona, then proceeds to accuse him of "insincerity," pointing to the fact that at the moment the play first appeared in Buenos Aires, the world had just witnessed the worst bloodbath of its history. That observation leads him to the conclusion that *La barca sin pescador* ". . . had to turn out antiquated from the moment of its debut, even from the moment of its conception. Certain things are born antiquated, old—all those that lack sincerity and sublimity."

J. Rodríguez-Richart, one of Casona's staunch defenders, answers Velloso neatly, pointing out several inaccuracies in his critique and negating most of his allegations. He readily acknowledges that Casona's plays lack sublimity, but makes the important point that sublimity rarely, if ever, characterizes *comedy*. It is almost a contradiction of terms. "Sublimity is rather more typical of Shakespeare, Racine, Schiller, Lorca—of tragedians in general. . . . To demand sublimity of a comedy is something like demanding cleverness of a tragedy."[28] He insists, moreover, that Casona's play does not lack sincerity.

> I don't regard the fact that a play is pleasant and agreeable as sufficient reason for calling it old or antiquated or retarded, even though it appeared shortly following the Second World War. Nor do I see any contradiction here. Besides the fact that in Argentina the devastation of that world tragedy probably had relatively little effect, it is perhaps appropriate to remember that during the period between 1939 and 1945, works such as *Ondine* and *The Madwoman of Chaillot* by Giraudoux; *Romeo and Jeanette* and *Leocadia* by Anouilh; *The Dead Queen* by Montherlant; *The Good Woman of Sezuan* by Brecht; *The Satin Slipper* by Claudel; *The Glass Menagerie* by Tennessee Williams . . . and many more . . . appeared, [none of which] has anything to do with the struggle that was unfolding when they made their appearance. Nor do I believe that there is any valid way of relating them to any essential aspect of that war. Can these works be classified as antiquated, retarded, or old at the moment of their debut? . . . Certainly they could have been in some way faithful to the concrete historical circumstances of the moment of their appearance, but this is not, as we can see, the only possibility for their survival, for the simple reason that a theatrical work does not acquire its permanent value by virtue of the current events that it reflects, but by its aesthetic components.[29]

Other critics, some more perceptive and sound than Velloso, nevertheless join him in his general opinion of *La barca sin pescador*. Velloso claims a high personal regard for Casona and his dramatic technique; so do Ricardo Doménech and Francisco Ruíz Ramón. In fact, there is a consensus of respect for Casona's ability to write plays that are theatrically acceptable. The clash, then, is clearly ideological and not aesthetic.

Doménech's diatribe against Casona's theater, unleashed in 1964, aroused a full-fledged polemic between Doménech and Luis Ponce de Leon. Doménech's article first appeared in *Insula* (#209, April 1964), and the crossfire between him and Ponce de León enlivened several issues of *Arriba* (Madrid, August 2, 12, 23); the whole package was later collected in Juan José Plans's *Alejandro Casona* (Oviedo, 1965, pp. 125–38). Charles H. Leighton identifies the bone of their contention succinctly: "Doménech condemns Casona for not being *engagé* while Ponce de León praises him for being *evasionista*" ("escapist"). Then he adds, with characteristic acuteness, "Casona is much too subtle to be classified as either."[30]

What, then, is Casona's theater, if not *engagé* or *escapist?* Appropriating the terminology devised by David Riesman et al (*The Lonely Crowd,* Garden City, N. Y., 1953), Leighton shows that Casona's hero is traditional, or other-oriented. Hence the difficulty that a typical *engagé* audience would find in grasping the appeal that Casona's plays still hold for those who refuse to surrender to social fundaments as the basis for all theater—and most criticism, for that matter. Mircea Eliade states the case for modern man:

Modern non-religious man assumes a new existential situation; he regards himself solely as the subject and agent of history, and he refuses all appeal to transcendence. In other words, he accepts no model for humanity outside the human condition as it can be seen in various historical situations. Man *makes himself,* and he only makes himself completely in proportion as he desacralizes himself and the world. The sacred is the prime obstacle to his freedom. He will become himself only when he is totally demysticized. He will not be truly free until he has killed the last god.

It does not fall to us to discuss this philosophical position. We will only observe that, in the last analysis, modern non-religious man assumes a tragic existence and that his existential choice is not without its greatness.[31]

Arnold Reichenberger puts it this way:

There seems to be a strange contradiction running through our world. Although this is a Christian society and Christianity is an optimistic religion with an untragic view of life, what we want to see on the stage and read in poetry or fiction is life seen or sensed as a mystery, with man struggling to unveil it, to fight his way *per aspera ad astra* on his own, rather than the uncritical acceptance of a dogmatically stated and authoritatively upheld answer. There seems to be a complete break between Sunday and the other six days of the week. What happens during the six days of the week provides the writer with dramatic and often tragic interest.[32]

Quite simply, Casona stands outside the current that carries the existential band wagon. He speaks for the still numerous traditionalists, or other-oriented audience. For such, Casona's plays represent anything but the tactics of "evasion" for which Ponce de Leon praises him and others berate him. It is hardly "evasion" to refuse to come to terms with death and persist in "old-fashioned" adherence to certain sacred models for humanity that exist beyond the baleful human condition.

Robert G. Hunter's *Shakespeare and the Comedy of Forgiveness* outlines with admirable thoroughness the Christian tradition that Casona follows in *La barca sin pescador*. Point by point, Hunter's explication of certain of Shakespeare's comedies applies just as handily to Casona's play. The antecedents of the secular comedy of forgiveness are the medieval mystery and morality plays, exhortatory allegories that seek to demonstrate man's relationship with God. In these early medieval plays, God frequently was a part of the "script," a member of the cast. His direct intervention—or the Virgin's—"was an automatic feature of the . . . play. Either He or the Virgin descends, surrounded by saints and angels, to prevent the punishment of the sinner on earth or to declare, as spectacularly as possible, the forgiveness of his sins in heaven."[33]

Hunter traces the conflict between mercy and justice through the form that came to be known as the debate of the Four Daughters of God, "an allegorical dramatization of the dialectic of divine mercy."[34] Justice, Truth, Mercy, and Peace debate man's case. Truth points out that to be consistent, God must punish inexorably. Mercy brings up man's repentance. Justice insists that God's sense of right (justice) knows no limits, hence the guilty must suffer without fail. Mercy avers that God's mercy is likewise infinite. Peace intervenes, granting that both arguments have their strengths, but she seems more inclined to favor mercy; she then suggests that the decision be left to God. Christ proposes the sacrifice, but no man or angel is capable of bringing it off, so the members of the Trinity counsel together and decide to send Christ himself to save man. All the virtues are reconciled.

Medieval literature, Hunter observes, reflected the duality of medieval man's attitude toward justice and mercy. "One should remember, in considering the medieval and sixteenth-century attitudes toward the problems of mercy and forgiveness, that, for the men of these periods, the virtue of justice was not noted for any admixture of benignity. Deeds of what seem to us abominable cruelty were regarded as praiseworthy when they were performed in justice's name."[35] Much of the harshness in the comedies of honor in Spain's Golden Age seems to hark back to the monolithic consideration of justice (equated with honor) with "no admixture of benignity." However, mercy was just as often presented in the same monolithic light. What is interesting is that the centuries have changed our views so slightly. There are mercy and justice advocates today, just as there were then.

Hunter cites both Aquinas and Luther to affirm that contrition makes God's mercy available to all men. "To say that in this life there is any sin of which one cannot repent is erroneous," says St. Thomas, "first, because this would destroy free will, secondly, because this would be derogatory to the power of grace."[36] This notion of infinite forgiveness informs more than just the medieval morality and mystery plays. It also characterizes much verse, such as Gonzalo de Berceo's devout *mester de clerecía*. It finally appears in a tradition of its own, the "comedies of forgiveness" of the Renaissance. These plays, however, do not directly explore the relationship of God to man; they have become completely secularized. But the same salutary, saving principles that make reconciliation possible between God and the sinning *humanum genus* also obtain in man's relationship to man. The Renaissance comedy of forgiveness, like so many morality and mystery plays before them, celebrate mercy rather than justice. If man would be forgiven, then he should be willing to forgive. The spectator is expected to see his own sinful state in the protagonist. The comedy of forgiveness, like the Spanish Golden Age plays, "follows the pattern from order disturbed to order restored,"[37] and order can be restored only along the lines of the Christian ethic.

But, insist the justice hounds, the sinner does not deserve to be forgiven. Hunter cites Dr. Johnson's disapproval of Shakespeare's *All's Well That Ends Well,* and Coleridge's rejection of Angelo in *Measure for Measure.* "I cannot reconcile my heart to Bertram," says Dr. Johnson. "A man noble without generosity and young without truth; who marries Helen as a coward, and leaves her as a profligate: when she is dead by his unkindness, sneaks home to a second marriage, is accused by a woman he has wronged, defends himself by falsehood, and is dismissed to happiness."[38] And Coleridge complains: "The pardon and marriage of Angelo . . . baffles the strong indignant claims of justice (for cruelty, with lust and damnable baseness, cannot be forgiven, because we cannot conceive of them as being *morally repented of*)."[39]

Essentially the same complaints echo in critiques of *La barca sin pescador* by L. W. Keats and Francisco Ruiz Ramón. Keats says: "A remorse-stricken Jordán finds the widow of Péter Anderson and falls in love with her and the simple life. We are left to understand that he will marry her, and that they will live happily ever after. . . . Plato says that the spirited element in man is recognized through the feeling of indignation, as, for example, when we are punished wrongly. My own gorge rises because Jordán is, wrongly, not punished."[40] Ruiz Ramón similarly complains, "The playwright obscures the social dimension of the conflict that he establishes in the first act through a tangential escape to an individual morality, which is, substantially, the negation of the consciousness of human solidarity and social responsibility. In *La barca sin pescador* no one assumes anything, no one redeems anything."[41]

Hunter recognizes that Johnson and Coleridge were respectable and competent, but were writing during a time when the dramatic tradition of Shakespeare's plays was outmoded. The best criticism seeks to understand the author fully, even if it means understanding what he owes to traditions that are no longer our own.[42] Ricardo Jordán, these critics have said, does not deserve to be forgiven. Keats goes on to grumble that "a . . . more fundamental objection is that Casona, by his treatment of Jordán, denies him liberty."[43] This places Keats in clear, direct opposition to St. Thomas, who, as we have seen, insists that "to say that in this life there is any sin of which one cannot repent, is erroneous, first because this would destroy free-will. . . ." Dr. Hunter suggests, ". . . to the Johnsonian objection that Bertram in *All's Well That Ends Well* does not deserve to be 'dismissed to happiness,' the medieval and Shakespearean answer would be the question, 'Who does?' And to Coleridge's statement that the 'pardon and marriage of Angelo [in *Measure for Measure*] . . . baffles the strong indignant claim of justice (for cruelty, with lust and damnable baseness, cannot be morally repented of)' the medieval and Shakespearean answer would be a flat, and probably rather shocked, denial."[44]

Hunter concedes that it is difficult not to share the doubts that arise in the face of unqualified forgiveness of an inveterate sinner, but if we insist on sitting in judgment and looking to the comedies of forgiveness for a "meting out of deserved rewards and punishments," we miss their point. The very horror of the protagonist's sins, says Dr. Hunter, should not alienate or shock us but should reassure us.[45] He cites the sins of incest, matricide, infanticide, patricide, and sacrilege to make the point that no sin is so great that mercy cannot intercede. He suggests that, since we are all sinners (and indeed the *humanum genus* figure of the comedy represents us), "unless God tempers his justice with mercy, we will all spend eternity in hell."[46]

Hunter suspects that modern man has moved even farther from the unqualified charity that Johnson and Coleridge failed to grasp in Shakespeare's plays.

Modern charity—if I may be permitted a massive generalization—is more likely to be associated with making allowances, with pity and tolerance. We tend to forgive the man who does evil not because we recognize ourselves in him, but because we see him as a poor unfortunate, a victim of heredity and environment, the creature of an unhappy past—one who, through no fault of his own, is our inferior. We are likely, therefore, in our contemplation of the *humanum genus* figure to react rather as the pharisee reacted to the publican. This is not the reaction which the sinning mortals of Shakespeare's comedies and of the medieval plays which preceded them were intended to provoke. Such dramas invite us to forgive the sins of others not because we (unlike them) are good, but because we (like them) are not good.[47]

Northrop Frye's commentary on types of "mythical movement" places comedy within the traditional formula of the happy ending.[48] Hunter asks the question, "Happy for whom?" and then answers his own question: "The ending of a comedy is happy because it pleases the characters of whom we, the members of the audience, approve."[49] The members of the audience expect to enjoy "a spectacle designed to convince [them], however momentarily, that beauty exists and that happiness and love are goals possible to attain."⁵⁰ For the happy ending expected of comedy, frustrating forces have to be defeated, and the characters identified with such forces likewise must suffer defeat. Casona's first act introduces several characters, all of whom he manages to make the audience dislike. Yet we come to identify with Ricardo Jordán; he is the *humanum genus*. But if he is going to have part in the anticipated happy ending, something must change. The author cannot grant felicity to a murderer and still have things end well.

The second act brings Ricardo and Estela together, developing a man/woman relationship that, for happy fulfillment, must point toward togetherness. Yet the man—the *humanum genus*—continues to be the frustrating force. So far, the audience has not approved of Ricardo, though the very fact that he is now in Estela's village shows certain changes that begin to soften his offenses. But the murder of Peter still stands between him and Estela; a union is impossible until all offense is erased.

Most theatergoers are not murderers, nor have they seriously entertained the thought. How then can Ricardo represent the *humanum genus* with whom we are expected to identify? Dr. Hunter explains it admirably:

The fulfillment of wishes is clearly one of the major functions of comedy, particularly romantic comedy. The comic dramatist creates a world in which the good things the spectator thinks he wants are possible of achievement. Love, beauty, and happiness exist in the worlds of comedy and they are gained by the people who inhabit those worlds. Now of all the wishes common to man, none is more poignant or more impossible of achievement than the desire to alter the past. There can be few humans who would not be pleased at the prospect of being able to undo something they ought not to have done but did anyway. There can be few more intense feelings of relief than those of the dreamer who, upon awakening from a nightmare, realizes that the horrors which were so vivid but a moment before do not in fact exist. It is this "sense of awakening from nightmare," as Northrop Frye calls it, that is communicated by the offender in the final scenes of the comedy of forgiveness when it is successful.⁵¹

Casona establishes the idea of Ricardo as the *humanum genus* in his method of introducing the play's theme. He instructs that the following notes should appear on all printed programs of the play:

Tradition's Legacy

In the most remote confines of China lives a fabulously rich Mandarin, whom we have never seen and of whom we know nothing. If, by merely pressing a button, we could cause his death and inherit his fortune without anyone's knowing about it, who among us would not press the button?

J. J. Rousseau

Then a greater bitterness assailed me. I began to consider that the Mandarin might have a large family who, deprived of the inheritance that I consumed on plates of richest china, would pass through all the traditional torments of human misery—days without rice, no clothing against the cold, charity denied them . . .

Eça de Queiroz

The question is, "Who among *us* would not press the button?" And Ricardo represents *us* as he lives out the consequences of his decision.

Repentance and Forgiveness

"One of the main concerns of the writer of secular comedies of forgiveness," says Hunter, "is the avoidance of crime, for the crimes which are pardoned in these plays invariably turn out to have been committed only in intention."[52] This states the case perfectly for Ricardo Jordán. His is a bloodless crime of will only, spawned by selfishness, to be sure. To awaken from his living nightmare, he can exercise his will to overcome that selfishness and create the *new man*.

Let us follow Ricardo step by step through the process of sin, repentance, and regeneration that identifies him as the *humanum genus*. First, the Devil himself (and who could speak with greater authority?) encapsulates Ricardo's past sinful life:

> *Gentleman.*—Your list is fat with betrayals, meanness, scandals, and injuries. Human misery has never moved you, you have never bothered to keep your word, and you have not respected your neighbor's wife. As for coveting your neighbor's property, it would be best not even to bring up the topic, don't you think?
>
> *Ricardo.*—Yes, that would be a long one . . .
>
> *Gentleman.*—To be concise, everything the law requires you to respect, you have violated; everything it forbids, you

have done. Up to now, only one commandment remains unbroken: "Thou shalt not kill."

Then he succeeds in getting Ricardo to add even the last sin to his list.

The next step in overcoming the audience's objections to the *humanum genus* and thus to effect the happy ending is to change Ricardo. St. Thomas has spelled out the three steps that lead to forgiveness: contrition, confession, and satisfaction. Notwithstanding the harshness of Ricardo's character heretofore, when he hears Estela's scream as she sees Peter fall over the cliff to his death, he enters the first step toward regeneration. We see the first feeble evidence of contrition, as he questions the Gentleman in black:

> *Ricardo.*—Wait . . . Who screamed?
> *Gentleman.*—What does that matter now?
> *Ricardo.*—Peter was not alone. I heard it perfectly . . . It was a woman's scream!
> *Gentleman.*—Don't ask. The less you know, the better off you'll be.
> *Ricardo.*—But that scream . . . If only I hadn't heard that scream . . . !

Then later in the same act, he asks his erstwhile "friends" (indeed the question is directed less toward them than toward himself), "What does it cost to silence the sound of a woman's scream in your ears? What river of gold can return light to those blue eyes after the stars have faded in them?"

His subsequent journey to the remote Nordic village where his victim's survivors live shows that contrition, or remorse, has brought him now to act. He comes in an attempt to soften the consequences of his deed and eventually confess his guilt. Estela meets him with unqualified—and unexpected—hospitality. He sits at her table, a table that suggests communion. Three are present there; Estela recites a portion of the Lord's Prayer. The fact that Ricardo is allowed to participate in this communion is leading. Though Estela is unable to end her prayer, declaring that she cannot forgive Peter's assassin, we have strong premonitions that the situation will improve.

Ricardo learns that Estela suspects Cristián, her brother-in-law. That is the moment for confession:

> *Ricardo.*—It is not you who must speak, Estela. I am the one to speak now. (He draws closer.) I came a great distance to tell you one thing; just one . . . and each time I tried to say it, a knot of fear and shame choked me.
> *Estela.*—If it's sad, don't say it. It's better to say good-bye as loyal friends.
> *Ricardo.*—I can't keep quiet any longer. I need to say it and you need to hear me.
> *Estela.*—(Instinctively afraid) Speak, then.
> *Ricardo.*—It has to do with Peter's death. (Estela looks away.) You said it that first day. God did not will that death. You were right, Estela. It was a man who did it. And that man is here!

Estela does not hear his confession, for he is not *materially* guilty. But she does forgive. The true murderer, Cristián, on the verge of death, asks for Estela's forgiveness. He too, we are told, has suffered for his guilt. When Estela returns from visiting him, she tells Ricardo:

> *Estela.*—I never imagined that one little word could have such power!
> *Ricardo.*—Forgive?
> *Estela.*—Forgive. It's hardly anything, yet it carries the kernel of a miracle inside it! I thought I could never say it, and when it fell from my lips like a ripe fruit, it wasn't only to Cristián that it gave peace. I myself suddenly felt cleaner, stronger, with all the knots untied.

She *does* forgive her husband's killer, and having forgiven Cristián, would certainly forgive Ricardo for his "lesser" sin of intention. Cristián's accident, timed to save Ricardo from ruining everything between him and Estela (Frye calls this moment the "point of ritual death"[53]), takes Estela offstage so that the Devil can come on. Ironically, the Devil turns out to be the angel who announces that a "ram" has been provided. Ricardo need not sacrifice his feelings. Cristián was the murderer after all.

The nightmare is over and we are washed with the relief we have expected from the beginning. What remains is the evidence of regeneration, or "satisfaction." Ricardo has experienced contrition, and has shown his willingness to confess (and if he did not make an actual confession, his will was sufficient, since, as the Devil himself affirms, "we are in the world of the will"). How does he now complete the demands of restitution? By honorably fulfilling his contract with the Devil!

> *Ricardo.*—(Thinking for a moment) What does that contract say?
> *Gentleman.*—The words are few, but they are very clear. "Ricardo Jordán agrees to kill a man."
> *Ricardo.*—Without blood.
> *Gentleman.*—Without blood.
> *Ricardo.*—Very well. The best way to liquidate a contract is to fulfill it. I have promised to kill and I will kill.
> *Gentleman.*—(Looking at him in surprise) Who?
> *Ricardo.*—The same one who signed that paper. Do you remember the day you came to my office? There you found a coward who was capable of any crime, as long as he didn't have to be around to witness it— a comfortable dealer in foreign sweat. A man capable of throwing entire harvests into the sea without thinking of the hungry workers who produced them. I've been struggling to conquer that man since I came here, and I'll continue to struggle for the rest of my life. And when there's no longer a single trace of him left in my soul, Ricardo Jordán will have killed Ricardo Jordán. Without blood! (The Devil drops his eyes in confusion.) Now we're *both* in the world of the will! You didn't expect it, did you?

Ricardo Jordán has been born again, as it were. The Devil, again the "angel" who brings tidings of felicity in the irony of the Casonian way, bids good-bye to Ricardo. "Good evening, Ricardo . . . Anderson." The Devil himself announces the *new man!*

The decidedly Christian overtones in this play find further

resonances in the symbolism represented by Estela. "It is upon the ability of women to suffer and forgive that Shakespeare builds his vision of an ideal romantic world," says Hunter. He could as well have spoken for Casona. The critic continues: "The romantic heroines, in a sense, replace Christ and his intermediary, the Virgin, as the forgivers of man's sins when the religious drama of the Middle Ages becomes the secular comedy of the Renaissance."[54] Clearly, Estela, the Virgin figure, represents love, the redeeming factor. The name itself means star, and one of the titles of the Virgin Mary is *Stella Maris,* the star of the sea.[55]

The lines of Tío Marko assume added significance in this regard. Together, he and Abuela discuss Ricardo's adjustment to the rustic village life he has adopted. Abuela praises Ricardo for his vast knowledge and the world he has seen. Tío Marko is totally unimpressed.

Marko.—Hold on there! That's where we part company. As a friend and companion, he's everything you could ask. But as for knowing, really *knowing,* he doesn't know up from around.

Abuela.—You're going to teach him, maybe?

Marko.—It wouldn't be the first time. Just this morning, when he saw poppies blooming in the roof moss, he asked me, serious as can be, who planted the flowers on the tile roof. Well, who do you think, sir? The wind!

Abuela.—Big deal! As if he didn't have more important things to keep in his head.

Marko.—Yeah, sure, plenty of schooling and books. But the truth is he can't even tell an ash from a birch tree; and he can't tell when a storm's coming by the flight of the gulls, nor how long before night falls by the bending of the grass. And to tell time, he has to go for his watch! You call that knowing? The one who knows is the watch!

Abuela.—Those are things from around here. People know the things of their own land . . .

Marko.—Yeah? Well, leave him alone at night in the forest and see if he can guide himself by the stars. Or maybe there are no stars in his country?

Abuela.—They might be different ones.

Marko.—(A little alarmed) Different? Are there different stars?
Abuela.—Well, that's what *I* say . . .
Marko.—(Immediately calm) Oh, all right, then. There may be other planets and other ways of speaking, because those are things that happen down here. But *nobody* moves the stars. The One who planted the polar star in the heavens knew what the fishermen needed.

In summary, *La barca sin pescador,* with its moral orientation, belongs to Casona's family of modern "Autos Sacramentales"; it upholds basic truths and makes a tacit plea for a more imaginative approach to life, especially in the face of our dehumanized social structure. The characters, as usual, are formed with uncanny dramatic insight, especially through the author's instinct for poetic compression in language.

La dama del alba (*The Lady of the Dawn*)

As the devil represents one of man's insoluble problems—the problem of evil—death likewise is one of the themes that perennially dog men's thoughts, and thus persists throughout the whole of Casona's theater. It is omnipresent, but not necessarily awesome and fearful, and indeed may be ". . . a comforter, a consoler, even a messenger of the Lord."[56] Life to Casona was more than mere happenstance, being fraught with purpose and divinely ordained. Thus, he is traditional in his view of death, believing, with the great majority of the Golden Age masters, that death represents a reward for some, condemnation for many. Gracián conveys this idea in his portrayal of death as an awesome queen, beautiful and desirable if viewed from one side, grotesque and frightening if viewed from the other. Casona recognized that death may be untimely and tragic, as the Pilgrim herself suggests when she states that she prefers never to be about when children are playing near the fire. Or it may be a peaceful, happy condition—a fulfillment.

The play unfolds in a small Asturian village, in the household of Martín Narcés. The heaviness of long-nurtured grief pervades the atmosphere of the home since Angélica, a few short days following her marriage to Martín, disappeared, apparently having drowned in the river that runs through the village. Despite

Tradition's Legacy

the urging of Abuelo (Grandfather), a wise patriarch, and Telva, the outspoken maid, Angélica's mother (Madre) refuses to allow her other children to attend school, for they would be forced to cross the river that took her daughter's life. An unexpected visitor comes to the house in the evening hours. It is the Peregrina (Pilgrim—Death), who has an assignment on this evening to meet Martín and take him with her. But, while playing with the children, she falls asleep, and Martín, instead of dying in an accident on horseback, as the Peregrina expected, saves a girl, Adela (who intended to commit suicide), from drowning in the river. The Peregrina is puzzled that her plans, so carefully outlined, could fail. By this time, Abuelo has recognized her, and fearing for the children, pleads with her to leave. She does so, but to Abuelo's consternation promises to return in seven months.

In those seven months, Adela wins the hearts of the whole family, including Madre. Martín falls in love with her, and it appears that she can totally replace Angélica. But Martín confesses to her that Angélica is not dead, that she eloped with another man three days after their wedding, a fact he has concealed from everyone. The Pilgrim hears this confession, for the time has come for her to return for someone in this household. However, it is not Adela she will take, but Angélica, who, long since abandoned by her lover, returns to salvage what she can of the life she rejected. She is met by the Pilgrim, who convinces her that she has no place here now, and accompanies her to the river, where the village folk will find her body a short while later.

Juan R. Castellano, in an article printed in 1952, points to Casona's propensity to depict features of his homeland in all his works, though the only play with a setting specifically in Asturias is *La dama del alba* (*The Lady of the Dawn*). In one of his letters, Casona expresses a yearning—then many miles and many years from satisfaction—to return to his province (*patria chica*): "Is it possible that the beautiful dream may finally be fulfilled, and that soon we may see each other again . . . in our homeland? I live only for that hope. Your personal case is different . . . , but I trust that, although it may be just in passing . . . , you will return to the soil of our infancy. . . ."[57] This yearning finds further expression in the dedicatory to *La dama del alba:* "To my homeland, Asturias; to her countryside, to her men, to her spirit." Joaquín de Entrambasaguas, speaking of Casona's characters, synthesizes what I have pointed out earlier regarding this aspect of his theater: ". . . The characters themselves are often symbols of the country, the sea . . . , symbols of Nature . . . with its vital completeness, opposed—following the Renaissance tradition—to the city, with its economic materialism, its deceit and perversity; as though mankind were to save itself . . . by gazing toward the abandoned serenity of Nature. . . ."[58]

The world of Asturias, whatever the author's purpose, is part of *La dama del alba*. The characters' words and expressions, and even the semi-ironic, half-skeptic, half-indulgent humor belong to that world. However, there are clearly two worlds in this play, the "real" one, filled with men and women of Asturias, their authentic language and spirit, and the supernatural world, present in the person of the Pilgrim. These two worlds interpenetrate, in baroque fashion. More simply, this interpenetration of the natural and supernatural is evident in the Pilgrim herself, whose characteristics are a blend of human warmth and supernatural allegory. Pablo de A. Cobos speaks briefly of the symbolism embodied in the names of Death in this play: "Death in the comedy has a generic name, Lady of the Dawn, and a specific name, Pilgrim. Lady of the Dawn is the most beautiful and optimistic of all the names that death uses to walk through the earth. Casona could choose no other; with it, he brings death up to date—the triumph of newborn morning over forgotten night. The name Pilgrim expresses the wandering condition of death, and even implies a sense of pity, which is never denied. Pilgrim comes into life like the Lady of Dawn comes into day."[59]

The setting of *La dama del alba* is appropriately timeless, as is the Pilgrim. Before she appears, she is announced by the incessant barking of the dog, able to sense intuitively the ominousness she brings. The general feeling she leaves with the adults is one of mystery and fear. The sagacious Abuelo seems to remember her, and the recollection plagues his mind, for though he is unable to recall for certain where or when he has met her, it does not seem to be a pleasant memory. He questions her at length: When has she been in the village before? She explains that she has come on several occasions, and names them. One of them was at the time of the tragic explosion in the mines, which took the lives of many of the village men. The Grandfather was there, injured, and he saw her among the dead—claiming her own. He remembers, and his immediate reaction is one of terror for his grandchildren, who were playing games with her a few moments before. He says to Telva, the servant, "Go up to them! Close all doors and windows! Warm them with your own body, if necessary! And regardless of who calls, let *no one* enter!" Alone with Pilgrim he says: "Look me in the eye and dare to say you don't know me. Do you remember the day the fire damp exploded in the mine? I was there, too, pinned beneath the debris with the acrid taste of smoke in my throat. You thought that my hour had arrived and you came too close. When, finally, the clean air entered the vein, I had already seen your pale face and felt your icy hands!" She does not deny her identity. The Abuelo begs her to leave his house, which she consents to do, but not without first explaining her position:

> *Pilgrim.*—. . . I am a good friend to the poor and to men of clear conscience. Why can't we talk like loyal friends?
>
> *Grandfather.*—I don't trust you. If you were loyal, you wouldn't enter houses in disguise to get into grief-filled rooms at the hour of the dawn.
>
> *Pilgrim.*—Who told you I need to enter? I'm always inside, watching you grow day by day from behind the mirrors.

She expresses here her timelessness. As life is eternally present, so, naturally, is death.

She explains that she once loved a child, and could not resist the temptation to express her love. The child is now an old man, a blind beggar, Nalón el Viejo.

> *Pilgrim.*—When he was a child he had the most beautiful glances that the world had ever seen; a blue temptation that attracted me from afar. One day I could not resist . . . and I kissed his eyes.

Grandfather.—Now he plays the guitar and begs at the village festivals with his dog and tin cup.

Pilgrim.—But I still love him as I did then! And some day I shall give him two stars to compensate for the harm my love has done him.

Her supernatural qualities are sometimes tragic, but she seems to possess power beyond the grave to repair the harm her love has caused.

Martín enters to interrupt the conversation between the Abuelo and the Peregrina, carrying the unconscious Adela. It is Martín whom the Peregrina wished to claim, but since she fell asleep and was unable to meet him at the appointed time, there is no longer any immediate danger. He has had an accident, but all that remains of the experience is a red spot on his temple, which the Peregrina gently removes. Adela regains consciousness, but is exhausted and soon faints again. The Abuelo casts an anxious, questioning glance at the Peregrina, who knows, by virtue of her supernatural perception, that Adela still lives; she assures the Abuelo that she is merely sleeping.

Martín was supposedly destined to die the night the Peregrina arrived, but Adela, who sought death, was not so destined. There is evidence of supernatural intervention by a power superior to that of the Peregrina. She is puzzled:

Pilgrim.—(*Pensive*) I don't understand. Someone intended to precipitate things that should mature in their own time. But what is in my books cannot be avoided. (*She starts to pick up her staff.*) I shall return.
Grandfather.—Wait. Explain those words to me.
Pilgrim.—It's difficult, because I don't see them too clearly, either. For the first time, I am facing a mystery that I don't quite understand. What power drove that girl on before her time?

For the first time, she has encountered a mystery she cannot comprehend—further definition of her supernatural character.

The Pilgrim explains that she is to visit this house and take with her a drowned girl, but not this night. "It's still seven months away." The Grandfather begs her to forget poor Adela, thinking that she will be the drowning victim, to which the

Tradition's Legacy

Peregrina answers, "Impossible. I don't give orders. I obey,"—another allusion to a power superior to her own. She returns as promised, to keep her rendezvous with "someone in this house," but still is uncertain for whom her visit is intended. Hearing of Angélica's infidelity as Martín confesses his love for Adela, the Pilgrim becomes certain of her mission, which she explains, symbolically, to the children:

> Pilgrim.—. . . One day the girl disappeared in the backwater. She had gone below, to live in the deep houses where fish knock on the window panes like cold birds; and the whole town called to her from above, but she did not hear. She was as though in a misty sleep, strolling through the moss gardens, her hair a floating wisp, her weightless hands a tender slowness. There she spent days, and years . . . Finally everyone began to forget her. Only her mother, her gaze steady, still waited . . . And finally, the miracle happened. One festive night—a night of bonfires and singing—the sleeping beauty was found, lovelier than ever. The water had respected her beauty, for her hair was clean, her hands still warm, and on her lips a smile of peace . . . as though the years below had been but an instant. (*The children are silent for a moment, impressed.*)
>
> Dorina.—What a strange story! When did it happen?
>
> Pilgrim.—It hasn't happened yet. But it is near . . . Don't you remember? Tonight all the rivers in the world carry water from the River Jordan!

She has prophesied exactly what will occur on this very night. When Angélica enters, the Pilgrim, without seeing her, senses her presence, recognizes her, and calls her by name. The Pilgrim proceeds to convince her of the futility of her position, which she is at first reluctant to accept. She exclaims, "No human force is capable of tearing me from this place!" Angélica is unaware of how profoundly true these words are. She tells the Pilgrim of her despair when her lover abandoned her, and the Pilgrim reads her thoughts:

> Pilgrim.—(*With a deeply suggestive tone, as though she were following aloud Angélica's thoughts.*) That night you thought that over there, on the other side of fear, is the country

of ultimate forgiveness, with a calm, white cold; where there is a peaceful smile for all lips, an infinite serenity for all eyes . . . and where it is beautiful to sleep, forever quiet, without pain and without end.

Angélica.—(*She turns, looking at her fearfully.*) Who are you that you know how to read my thoughts?

Angélica continues to protest until the Pilgrim convinces her, in a scene that expresses poetically the facet of death we shall consider shortly—death as a fulfillment.

Pilgrim.—I'll show you the way. Come with me, and tomorrow the town will have its legend. (*She takes her by the hand.*) Shall we?

Angélica.—Let go . . . There's something about you that frightens me.

Pilgrim.—Still? Look at me carefully. How do you see me now?

Angélica.—(*Contemplating her, fascinated.*) Like a great, startled dream . . . But more and more beautiful . . .

Pilgrim.—There is the whole secret! First live passionately, then die beautifully! (*She places the crown of roses in her hair.*) There . . . as though you were going to a wedding . . . Courage, Angélica . . . One moment of courage, and your memory will be rooted in the village like an oak full of nests. Shall we?

Angélica.—(*Closing her eyes.*) Yes.

The village people find her in the river, serene in death, as the Peregrina foretold. Everyone accepts Angélica's reappearance as a miracle, and another of the Pilgrim's predictions is fulfilled.

Casona does not sacrifice characterization to the symbolic nature of the Pilgrim. She possesses human qualities that redeem her from the purely allegorical. When she first appears, she has not lost her way, but "the strength to travel it"; she is tired and cold. At length, the children ask her if she knows any games. She answers that she has forgotten them all, but adds, ". . . if you teach me, I can learn." She begins to play, and soon discovers the miracle of laughter, but finds difficulty in controlling it. Her laughter increases in almost frenzied crescendo, until a convulsive burst frightens the children, and she herself is astonished: "What am I doing? What is this that swells in my throat and reverberates in my mouth with the ring of crystal?" Though unaccustomed to such merriment, she is capable of it; but it soon tires her, and she finds that she must rest, even falling asleep, leaving instructions that she be awakened promptly at nine o'clock. She is fallible, for she oversleeps, and Martín, whom she was to meet, is spared. "Only a child could accomplish such a miracle," she declares. This expression reflects a human tenderness. "Children are good friends of mine," she says. Later, during the festivities of the Noche de San Juan, Andrés, the youngest child, exclaims, "I'm going to jump over the bonfire like the big guys! Will you come with us?"—to which she answers, "No. When children jump over fires, I would prefer never to be there."

Aware of the terror that people feel for her, and distressed, she desires understanding and longs to feel welcome. She tells the Abuelo, who has invited her to leave, "I only wish, before I leave, that you should bid me good-bye without hatred, with a kind word." Her love and her emotions are tragic, as she herself explains:

I too should like to adorn myself with roses like the peasant girls, live among happy children and have a beautiful man to love. But when I go to cut roses, the whole garden freezes. When children play with me, I have to turn my head for fear that they will remain still when I touch them. And as for men, what good does it do me that the handsomest of them come looking for me on horseback? When I kiss them I feel their useless arms slide limply from my waist. (*Desperately*) Do you understand now the bitterness of my destiny? To witness all grief without being able to cry . . . To have all the sentiments of a woman without being able to use any of them . . . To be condemned to kill always, always, without ever being able to die! (*She falls, overwhelmed, into the armchair with her forehead between her hands.*)

Noting her emotion, the Abuelo is moved:

    (. . . *He draws near and puts his hand gently on her shoulder.*)
    Grandfather.—Poor woman.

Pilgrim.—Thank you, Grandfather. I asked you for a little understanding and you have called me a woman, which is the most beautiful word on a man's lips.

She is capable of warm gratitude, and delights in her qualities of womanhood, even though unable to express them. At one point, she even contemplates herself in Adela's mirror with "feminine curiosity," providing another example of Casona's impeccable equilibrium in blending the worlds of the natural and the supernatural.

The Pilgrim's assertion that she is a good friend to the poor and to men of clear conscience points toward the aspect of death that Casona prefers to emphasize. When Grandfather accuses her of being cruel and treacherous, she responds, "When men push me against each other, yes. But when you allow me to come at my own pace . . . how tenderly are the final knots loosed! And how peaceful are the smiles at the edge of dawn!" She later points out that the mystics awaited her coming with ecstatic impatience, poets sang to her as to their love, and the greatest Spanish wise man [Seneca] called her "liberty."

It is quite in keeping with Casona's idea of death as a fulfillment that he should choose a woman—with all the instincts of her femininity—as the personification of death. A masculine personage could scarcely represent the blend of tenderness and resolution that Casona distills into this personality.

The author's position is also reflected in *La casa de los siete balcones* (The house of the seven gables), a play we shall treat in a later chapter. Uriel, a mute, and one of the principal characters in that play, can on occasion find respite from the painful sordidness that surrounds him only through the visits he receives from three characters now on the other side of death's mystery. Mother (Madre), Grandfather (Abuelo), and Alicia, all dead for several years, return to comfort him. They appear dressed in immaculate white, a suggestion of purity (contrasted with the archetypal image of death represented in black). Their movements are never hurried, and they give the illusion of perfect peace. When Uriel joins them, he says, "I didn't even realize . . . How can it be so incredibly easy? How is it possible for me suddenly to feel so free and calm?" (*OC,* 2:947). Earlier, before finding this peace, he tries to persuade Alicia to reveal to him how to pass over into the next world, and their dialogue is a beautifully poetic expression of death's fulfillment:

> *Uriel.*—There must be a hidden passage . . . a secret door . . . , something! How did you do it?
> *Alicia.*—Without realizing it. I only remember that it was on a beach. Between the rocks on the ocean bed I could see a sea star. I had never seen anything more beautiful! But it was down so deep, so deep . . . I thought I would never reach it. Have you ever seen a sea star?
> *Uriel.*—No.
> *Alicia.*—Look at it. Isn't it lovely?
> *Uriel.*—Lovely, yes. But what happened then . . . when you reached it?
> *Alicia.*—Nothing. I stayed there calmly on the bottom, and it began to grow dark.
> *Uriel.*—And the darkness didn't frighten you?
> *Alicia.*—Why should it? I had a star all my own.

Those of us still "over here where all the questions are" may resent Casona's untimely encounter with his own private Pilgrim, but must concede that "death is more skillful than we" and find comfort in the hope that he, now "over there, where the only answer is,"[60] has found in his union with the Pilgrim the fulfillment he expected.

Chapter Three
Fantasy versus Reality

Much of what has been written to define Casona's theater deals with his proclivity for fantasy and fantastic situations. One such treatise is Charles H. Leighton's article "Alejandro Casona's 'Pirandellism,'" which appeared in *Symposium* 17 (1963). Pirandello has become, it seems, one of the principal spokesmen for the twentieth century, against whom it is commonplace to measure other writers,[1] probably because of his total surrender to solipsism.[2] Mr. Leighton's article concludes that "Casona rejects both the Pirandellian theses and the Pirandellian solution." While Pirandello's plays, like Benavente's, are cast in the conventional bourgeois mold, his thesis is that illusion is indispensable in life. Conversely, Casona creates a world of true fantasy with unusual situations—Dr. Ariel's retreat for suicides in *Prohibido suicidarse en primavera,* his aid station for sick souls in *Los árboles mueren de pie,* Ricardo's fantastic republic in *La sirena varada*—and these often add supernatural characters. But his thesis is that man is obliged to strive for the acquisition of truth, difficult as it is to apprehend. The principal avenue for its apprehension is love, and love requires total honesty.

So we return again to the task of discovering Casona's position on the solipsistic scale, a question central to his *Weltanschauung,* and hence to the aesthetic understanding of his theater. As Leighton points out, Casona is a kindred spirit of Cervantes in that he recognizes the difficulty mortals have in apprehending truth, but does not therefore excuse man in his quest for it, for he does believe that it exists.[3] His liberal use of fantasy in no way belies this belief; on the contrary, Casona clearly allows that there are many truths beyond the normal range of our senses, truths which are to him a "poetic" reality. His essay "¿Brujas otra vez?" (Witches again?) expresses these views:

Is it true, sir, that you don't believe in witches? No, of course you don't. You are up-to-date, born in an asphalt civilization, accustomed

Fantasy versus Reality

to having things function by themselves at the touch of a button. You worry only about the great themes of our time, from atomic disintegration to astronautical voyages. In short: you, with your electric buttons everywhere, your weekly radiations and thermonuclear explosions that you read about in your newspaper, live surrounded by mysteries that even the men who manipulate them are incapable of explaining. But believe in witches—by no means! You are proud of your technical mysteries, but poetic mysteries make you blush. You have exchanged the old artistic witchcraft for a new scientific witchcraft, and culturally, you think you have made a bargain. Pardon me if I don't congratulate you.[4]

Such a position has led many critics to brand Casona's production with the epithet of "evasionism," a label he rejects rather decisively:

I do not agree with the term "evasionism," which some critics, many in good faith, have so cheerfully thrust upon me like an inquisitor's judgment. I am not an "escapist" who closes his eyes to surrounding reality, thinking to nullify it with the naive measure of not looking at it. The fact is simply that I do not consider anguish, desperation, negation and sex the only realities. I believe that dreams are another reality, just as "real" as wakefulness; I believe that a teardrop from one in love is as humanly respectable as any drop of sweat; and I believe that the vast majority of truths that allow us to heal a wound or reach the moon we owe, in the first place, to our marvelous capacity for fantasy. Menéndez Pidal wrote once that, for the Spaniards, besides the immediate and common reality, there exists a second reality, charged with wonder, an "extraordinary" reality that appears first in *Poema del Cid*, then in the *Romancero*, and bursts forth in all its splendor in the *Quijote*. If what my critics intended was to include me in this second marvelous and very Spanish reality, my heartfelt thanks.[5]

Armed thus with Casona's own reasoning, let us see how dramatically these views unfold.

La sirena varada (Mermaid aground)

Ricardo, young, rich, and bored, has rented an isolated mansion where, as a reaction against the rigidity of his childhood education, he plans to build an extravagant republic devoid of common sense. He points out to Don Florín, a longtime family friend who tries to dissuade him from his wild notions, that he has already succeeded in attracting one constituent, Daniel, a painter who wears a bandage over his eyes to "discover new colors." Moreover, Pedrote, the servant, also mentions that they are living with a ghost—it was part of the bargain when Ricardo rented the house. And Ricardo has invited another rare specimen to join their group and preside over it, Papa Samy—a circus clown whom Don Florín met years earlier, and whose daughter, now supposedly dead, Ricardo once saved from drowning. Don Florín is even less impressed with Ricardo's project when the "ghost" appears and explains that he has inhabited the house for some four years, "haunting" it to keep people away so that he could cultivate his garden and live in peace. Ricardo reacts unsympathetically, convincing the poor ghost—Don Joaquín—that he really *is* a ghost, that he is Napoleon.

At this point, Pedrote appears to announce that a shadow is climbing up the vines toward one of the windows. The "shadow" proves to be the beautiful but incoherent Sirena, who claims to be a siren and professes her love for Ricardo. The latter, momentarily shaken, yields shortly to her enticing beauty. Florín suspects that Sirena is in some way allied with Samy, probably for the purpose of laying hold on Ricardo's fortune. Ricardo at first resists this reasoning, but later, when Samy discloses that Sirena is his insane daughter (the same person whom Ricardo saved from drowning years earlier), he surrenders to Florín's plea to return to the world of reason, and begs him to cure her of her insanity. Florín is singularly successful with both Sirena and Ricardo until Pipo, the circus impresario, reveals to Ricardo what Samy has already confessed to Florín: Pipo has possessed Sirena for some months, taking brutal advantage of her derangement. He offers to withdraw for a price. Ricardo faces him with cold determination and forces him to leave, but the situation precipitates an excitement in him that leads him to tear the bandage from Daniel's eyes. The discovery that Daniel is blind is too impressive for Ricardo, still unstable, who proceeds to undo the work that Florín has accomplished, attempting to drive Sirena back to her madness. But this time, Sirena herself holds him to reality. For the sake of the child she is going to have, she refuses his offer to take her "back to the sea."

Thus the relevancy of Leighton's thesis is clear: where Pirandello generally justifies his characters in their illusions, Casona's characters are led to realize that their illusions are mere escapes from life's problems, not solutions to them. "Love needs the truth," says Don Florín. And so it would seem, for Ricardo, once he realizes he loves Sirena, insists upon knowing her identity. "If I thought of you today as I did that first day, I would ask for nothing but makebelieve to be happy with you. But . . . now I love you. Love you for real." For Casona, love transcends illusion; for Pirandello, love seems to depend upon it. Conclusive as the foregoing observations seem, however, there is still some doubt. What of the tragic Daniel? We find no answer to his pathetic question, "What harm did [my bandage] do you?" Is he not, after all, entitled to the little comfort he can find from his blindfold, pretending that it is there for a purpose other than the one it serves? Perhaps not. Perhaps we should accept at face value Don Florín's suggestion, "no matter how harsh the truth is, one should face it squarely." And *love,* not *illusion,* will make the truth bearable. But let us explore the question further.

Los árboles mueren de pie (Trees die standing)

Los árboles mueren de pie reveals the same general ideology, but a rather less decisive affirmation in favor of reality as opposed to illusion. Dr. Ariel, a philanthropist, has established a charity institution for sick souls. To this rare establishment comes a young lady, Marta, who was saved from suicide when someone threw a bouquet of roses and a slip of paper into her window with the word *mañana* printed on the paper. The following morning, she found a note, which someone had slipped under her door, inviting her to this place. Arriving at about the same time is Balboa, whom Dr. Ariel has sent with his personal recommendation. Both Marta and Balboa are more than a little disconcerted by the incoherent, often sinister activities about them, having no notion of what the place is. Mauricio, the Director, rescues them from their frustration, explaining to Marta that the purpose of his organization is to "arrive at charity by the path of poetry"—to give hope to the hopeless. He persuades Marta to become a part of their organization. Meanwhile Helena (Mauricio's secretary) has explained the same details to Balboa, who in turn puts his problem to Mauricio: his grandson, whom he and his wife, the Abuela, had raised with unwise indulgence, left home on a night when Balboa, surprising him in the act of breaking into his safe, struck him and ordered him out. The Abuela, while she has not reproached her husband openly, has shown with her silence how deeply her grandson's absence has affected her. Balboa, knowing his grandson to be an inveterate criminal, began to write letters to the Abuela, signing their grandson's name. In his merciful deceit, Balboa has "reformed" his grandson, who supposedly is now an architect, married, and working in Canada. Unfortunately, Balboa explains, the real grandson ruined the game by sending a cable stating that he would be home soon for a visit on the ship *Saturnia*. But the *Saturnia* sank, with all her passengers, on the high sea. Balboa, who cannot bring himself to destroy his wife's hopes with the news of their grandson's death, begs Mauricio to take the part of the grandson, visit their house, and bring some hope to the failing old lady. Intrigued and challenged, Mauricio hesitates because he has no one to play the part of the wife. Then he thinks of Marta. Both Mauricio and Balboa are sure that she will do splendidly.

Mauricio and Marta (now called Isabel) transcend many difficulties, successfully deceiving the Abuela until the real grandson appears. He had not been aboard the ill-fated *Saturnia* but had taken another vessel under an assumed name. Hoping to appeal to a sense of decency and gratitude he no longer possesses, Mauricio reveals to him their charitable masquerade, but instead of agreeing to go along the grandson threatens to expose them to the Abuela unless they can produce the sum of two hundred thousand pesos, needed to redeem him from threatened gang reprisal. Of course, they cannot. And Balboa will not accede to his suggestion that he sell the house, which the Abuela loves. So the grandson goes to the Abuela, who meanwhile has exacted a confession from Balboa. Recognizing her grandson to be the complete reprobate that he is, she too refuses him the money and turns him out. Mauricio and Marta-Isabel do not know that the Abuela is informed of their part in the drama, so she in turn acts out a part of her own, refusing to allow them to suspect that they have failed. She sends them away happily deceived, as she was originally.

Fantasy versus Reality

The story supports claims that Casona generally subordinates the dubious merits of illusion to reality. He seems to be in full sympathy with the functionaries of Dr. Ariel's institution who complain of the impersonal number-identification system, which replaces the individuals' given names. And the following lines leave the impression that the truth, however harsh, should be faced squarely:

> *Isabel.*—You can still do some good here. This is your last chance. Confess to the Abuela the whole truth.
>
> *Mauricio.*—What good would that do?
>
> *Isabel.*—It's like taking off a bandage. You can do it little by little, with your soul in your fingertips. Don't wait for him to tear it off with a jerk.
>
> *Mauricio.*—I can't. I wouldn't have the courage. I don't want to look at a wound that I myself have helped to cause and can no longer heal. Let's get out of here as soon as possible!
>
> *Isabel.*—To your quiet, comfortable house, to amuse ourselves inventing dreams that turn out like this? No, Mauricio; you go alone.
>
> *Mauricio.*—You surely don't intend to stay here!
>
> *Isabel.*—I wish I could. But I don't want to leave this make-believe world to go back with you to another just as false as this one.
>
> *Mauricio.*—Where, then? Do you intend to go back to what you had before?
>
> *Isabel.*—It seems incredible, doesn't it? And yet that is the great lesson I have learned here. My room was narrow and poor, but I didn't need any more; it was just my size. In the winter, the cold would come in through the window, but it was a clean cold which wrapped itself around me like a housecoat. And there were no roses in the window; just some dust-covered geraniums. But it was all my size, and all mine: my poverty, my cold, my geraniums.

Mauricio's well-planned deception has failed, while the old Abuela's improvised scheme succeeds. Mauricio, this time the deceived rather than the deceiver, will no doubt never be the wiser. The audience yearns for the old lady, wishing that Mauricio could have brought it off. Juan R. Castellano has approached briefly this topic in a short article entitled "Mi última conversación con Alejandro Casona," wherein the question of illusion versus reality is once more raised: "In 1925 a work [by Nicolai Evréinov] was presented which I have not yet read, *The Foundation of Happiness.* I have read, on the other hand, another of his plays, *The Chief Thing;* in its preface the author says something that cannot help but remind us of Casona. In one place he writes: 'Since we are unable to give happiness to the unfortunate, we must at least give them the illusion of happiness,' and elsewhere he adds: 'We never live in the present. We live in the past and in the future, and in our thought we recreate the one as well as the other . . . And we hardly know what is more real, more important for us—that which really happened or that which we invented.' "[6] Can we be as conclusive in our judgment of Casona's approach as other critics have been?[7] Let us withhold our final evaluation of this problem until we have examined one more of Casona's plays.

Prohibido suicidarse en primavera
(Suicide prohibited in springtime)

The scene is a rare sanitarium—a suicide home established, again, by Dr. Ariel. Its function, ostensibly, is to *facilitate* suicide. To this institution have come several potential suicides: a "lover" who claims to have had a long affair with the lovely opera singer, Cora Yako; a professor of philosophy who throws himself into the lake each morning but inevitably swims out again; and a Dama Triste (Sorrowful lady) who feels alienated from the material world. Dr. Roda, the director, and Hans, his assistant, are discussing the patients when the curtain opens. Shortly, Alicia, who has heard of the Suicide Home, enters, screaming, from the "Galería del Silencio." Her intentions were to kill herself, but at the last minute she recognizes the folly of such an act, and Dr. Ariel persuades her to join his staff.

Then Fernando and Chole, both reporters, appear, having stumbled onto the place by accident. They are determined to find a human-interest story to publish in their newspaper. Dr. Roda does not deny them information; in fact, he explains to them the real purpose of the institution. Its founder designed it as a refuge for individuals desperate enough to take their own lives. The patients, finding everything at their disposal to facilitate death, are no longer intrigued by it; death no longer represents for them an escape from reality because it has become a reality. In constant contact with the beauties of nature, they are gradually cured. After offering this explanation, Dr. Roda asks Fernando and Chole—two "perfectly happy" individuals—to serve as his assistants for a brief period. They accept.

While Fernando and Chole are attending to their new duties, Juan, Fernando's brother, arrives and attempts to shoot himself. Hans barely manages to deflect the pistol in time. Juan's problem, he explains, is that despite his struggles, he never succeeds, while Fernando, who has robbed him of all his triumphs, succeeds without effort at everything. Juan, who fears that his jealousy will lead him to fratricide, prefers to kill himself. Shortly, another personality appears. Not seeking to do away with herself, but knowing the value of publicity, she comes to enhance her image. This is the opera singer Cora Yako, with whom the "imaginary lover" claims to have had an affair. Upon learning of his "devotion," Cora pursues him almost savagely.

Chole soon discovers Juan's motive for attempting suicide, and also learns that she unwittingly plays a significant role in his tragedy: he is in love with her. Impulsively concluding that if she is out of the way, the brothers will come together, she rushes to the lake and throws herself in, but Juan saves her. Meanwhile Cora Yako offers the Amante Imaginario (Imaginary Lover) a chance to go away with her and see all the places he has dreamed of. To be sure, there are a number of unpleasantries he has never considered—consuls, mosquitos, exotic diseases, . . . and a possessive female. He does not go with her but accepts instead Fernando's offer to work on his newspaper staff, in charge of the section "Viajes y Aventuras," although he has never traveled and has just been through his only significant adventure. Fernando observes, "Art is not a question of experience; it is a question of imagination."

Chole, following her brush with death, and sensing the injustice of Juan's deprivation, resolves not to go away with Fernando but to stay with Juan. "Let there be in his life at least the illusion of womanhood," she says. Juan, recognizing that she does not really love him, and seeing finally that Fernando too suffers, rejects Chole's offer. She and Fernando leave together, their happiness deepened and tempered now by their greater understanding of human suffering. After they have gone, Juan retrieves his pistol from the desk as Alicia comes in with a cheerful greeting, persuading Juan to give her the pistol, which she will throw into the lake. The two exit together.

Chole's words, "Let there be in his life at least the illusion of womanhood," recall what we have already cited from Nicolai Evreinov. However, Juan realizes that he would not be content with only the illusion of womanhood, and his rejection of Chole's offer to remain with him is a courageous confrontation of reality. And life, if one has enough faith in it, says Dr. Roda, will eventually offer a marvelous surprise. So it happens with Juan. The fact that he and Alicia exit together is pregnant with the implication of better things for both of them.

But the main question of illusion versus reality in this drama revolves about the Imaginary Lover, who, refusing to face the tedium of impersonality in his bank-clerk existence, imagines that Cora Yako, while playing Margarita in *Faust,* sings solely for him. Her eyes, he says, turned constantly toward his seat in the gallery. The following night, when she sang the lead in *Madame Butterfly,* the phenomenon repeated itself. The next day, the Lover took enough money from the bank to buy her a bouquet of orchids, but later, full of illusion, went backstage to meet her and saw his orchids carelessly discarded in a corner, the card unopened. His dream shattered, he resolves to commit suicide, but does not confess his true motive; instead, he tells everyone of his "adventures" with the beautiful opera star. After Cora actually appears and the imaginary lover becomes a real lover, he understands that the dream was far more beautiful than the reality: "Since we are unable to give happiness to the unfortunate, we must at least give them the illusion of happiness." Moreover, fantasy triumphs again in the Lover's decision to accept the job Fernando offers him. He will employ his imagination to provide pleasure for those countless readers who have never had the opportunity to travel. It does not really matter that he himself has not had that opportunity. "Art is not a question of experience. It is a question of imagination."

In summary: Ricardo's project in *La sirena varada* fails because he is, after all, as implacable, as inhuman in his quest for an imaginative world as the world is in its indifference. He tyrannically forces Don Joaquín to believe he is actually dead, that he is Napoleon. Ricardo's inhumanity and lack of restraint doom him to failure. In *Los árboles mueren de pie,* Mauricio, whose purpose is noble, also lays aside some basic human considerations as he institutionalizes hope. He forces upon his personnel an impersonal number-identification system and considers art superior to life.[8] But it is the human element that defeats him. Marta-Isabel, unable to divorce her own sentiment from the role she is supposed to play, becomes attached to the Abuela and falls in love with Mauricio; and he, in turn, though he considers himself above becoming emotionally involved in his game of make-believe, falls in love with Marta-Isabel. The reality they wish to conceal from the Abuela (the profligate grandson) appears, and Mauricio is helpless against him. On the other hand, Abuela succeeds in her deception, but for her it is not a game as it was at first for Mauricio; she is not serving art, but humanity. She is motivated only by her desire to see the young couple happy. Marta-Isabel, who has never known true happiness, is allowed the joy she can find with Mauricio, and the "illusion of happiness" in her faith that the Abuela has believed them. The Imaginary Lover in *Prohibido suicidarse en primavera* chooses to make a living out of his dreams. But his illusion is not destructive; he faces the truth to the extent that he admits that he has never traveled, and that his work depends not upon experience but imagination. And there lies the key: Casona would justify illusion only insofar as it is edifying. He would no doubt agree with Socrates that the Good, the True, and the Beautiful are synonymous.

Strengths and Weaknesses

The close connection that exists between modern references to solipsism and the Pirandellian question prompted the excellent article we have quoted by Charles Leighton wherein the author suggests that besides the differences in ideology between Casona and Pirandello, there are also differences of form. Eric Bentley says of Pirandello's works:

A first reading of his forty-four plays leaves us with an impression of monotony. A second reading calls our attention to grave faults in dramatic structure and grave limitations in character portrayal. One of the most frequent plays performed in Italy, *Tutto per bene,* has a central scene of the rankest ham melodrama. Two that are translated into English and have been highly praised (*Henry IV* and *The Pleasure of Honesty*) have an expository first act of such cumbersome explanatoriness that one would think the author a plodding mediocrity or a careless hack. Over-all structure? Pirandello forces all his full-length plays into the three-act mold whether they really fit it or not. Sometimes he has obvious difficulty . . . in making the material spin out. More often one simply remains uncertain about the relation of act to act.[9]

No such criticism could apply to Casona's works. To be sure, his plays have weaknesses. For example, the number of coincidental occurrences in *Prohibido suicidarse en primavera* strains credibility. Juan's arrival happens to coincide with the fortuitous visit of Fernando and Chole to the suicide home; Cora Yako arrives in time to encounter her "Lover"; the "Padre," seeking solace for the loss of his daughter, Alicia, happens to find the other Alicia, whose appearance is so like his daughter's that he is immediately consoled. Moreover, there is a breach in consistency when Hans, who is so eager to see a suicide consummated that he is able to stand by and observe while Chole throws herself into the lake, deflects Juan's pistol so that he does not succeed in killing himself. Then there is the overriding sentimentality, which perhaps causes some of Casona's works to share the opprobrium Bentley describes for *Tutto per bene.* To the Spanish mind, more accustomed to overt emotional reactions than the Anglo-Saxon, a critical view of this tendency may have little validity. Casona's words, "I believe that a teardrop from one in love is as humanly respectable as any drop of sweat," partially justify him in this regard. But audiences in the United States generally require somewhat greater restraint.

Casona's strong points easily transcend such weaknesses. The opening scenes of *Los árboles mueren de pie* are an expository masterpiece representative of Casona's remarkable sense of timing and suspense. The setting offers the first suggestions of enigma: the spectator finds himself in a large modern office, with furnishings of the usual variety, but with puzzling artifices strewn about that seem completely incongruous with the businesslike appearance of the office: ". . . fishing nets, wire masks, a headless mannequin with a cloak, a world globe, useless firearms,

Fantasy versus Reality

colored maps of countries that have never existed—all the motley promiscuity of an auction sale or an antique shop." This setting creates a mood of fantasy and prepares us, partially, for the activities to follow. The initial dialogue between the secretary Helena and the Typist, so significant for exposition yet so whimsically elusive, serves further to establish the air of mystery about the place. When the Typist, referring to Mauricio, uses the word "Boss" (*Jefe*), Helena corrects her incisively. "Boss" might give the wrong impression. "Director" is the correct term. Her next statement suggests a possibility of some illegal procedure: "Many lives depend upon us, but the road is full of dangers. We could just as easily deserve the gratitude of humanity as wind up in jail this very night." The admonition, "Get used to obeying without question," tends to solidify the suspicion. The question of the files of various colors and categories is another mystery, meaningful only when the entire picture is disclosed.

It seems incredible that so many varied events can occur without revealing the actual purpose of the institution. The Protestant Pastor, "too perfect to be real," enters protesting. He is a linguist of considerable accomplishment, a man who has studied for forty years. The same imperative suggestion is reiterated to him: "You either obey unquestioningly or get out of the program." He resigns himself with a feeble complaint: "Oh, well . . . anything for the cause." But what is their cause? They do not use their own names because, "what would happen if one of our group, through some blunder, should fall into the hands of the police? The whole organization would be exposed!" By now the spectator is almost certain that the enterprise is dedicated to some illicit pursuit.

The Illusionist, another of several characters of the first act, also has a mild complaint for which he is reprimanded. He manages to answer:

> *Illusionist.*—I was just asking.
>> *Helena.*—(Authoritatively) Not even that! The door is open to anyone who is not willing to give himself to the cause with his whole soul. He will only be requested upon leaving to keep the same pledge that was requested upon entering: absolute silence.

The Illusionist's eccentric activities only broaden the mystery. After he exits, Isabel makes her entrance, followed by Balboa. They, of course, are as puzzled as the audience. The further mention of "opium smoker" and "kidnapped children" suffices to affirm audience suspicions regarding the illegality of the establishment. The Pastor admonishes Balboa and Isabel to get out while there is still time, implying that the organization has some sinister hold on him. The Mendigo (Beggar) appears, a sordid figure, "a fugitive from 'The Court of Miracles,' with a grimy romantic cape, a broad felt hat and a patch over one eye," and temporarily disconcerts the two clients—and the audience—with the following activities:

> He goes quite naturally, without paying any attention to them, to the table, where he deposits on a silver platter varied objects he takes from his deep pockets: a pearl necklace, several watches with chains, and some pocketbooks. Then he dials an extension number.
>
> *Mendigo.*—Hello. SS-2 here. Mission accomplished. No complications. No, don't worry, no one followed me. . . .

Spectators must believe, with Balboa, that they are in the middle of the Mafia. But thereupon the Hunter enters with a pair of dogs, makes a telephone call, orders three-dozen rabbits and fifty hunting dogs, and departs abruptly. Little wonder that Balboa is confused! "Not a sect, nor a lodge, not the Mafia. But what, then?" The only plausible explanation is the one offered by Isabel: "Haven't you heard of the case of that asylum where all the inmates revolted, tied up all the nurses and took over their jobs? We've fallen into a band of madmen!"

What could contribute more to explain the fantastic nature of such an organization for sick souls than this series of disconnected scenes? Mauricio enters, declaring: "The only thing that I hasten to clarify is that nothing you might have suspected up to now is true. You are not among kidnappers, nor ruffians, nor madmen." He then proceeds to explain the organization, and by now the spectator is ready to accept anything. No explanation could be too incredible after the barrage of events witnessed up to this point.

One very important factor in Casona's dramatic art, the one

that most readily offsets his tendency toward sentimentality and absorbs whatever antipathy such a tendency may arouse in certain critics, is his impeccable sense of the comic. Let us follow a sampling of his humor in each of these three plays. In *La sirena varada,* the Ghost, Don Joaquín, provides delightful comedy:

> *The Ghost enters, solemn in his white vesture, and crosses the stage slowly toward the opposite exit.*
> *Florín.*—. . . What kind of prank is this?
> *Ricardo.*—Shhh! Good evening, Mr. Ghost. What, leaving already? Wait, sit down a moment.
> *Fantasma.*—(*Solemn and disdainful*) Miserable mortal!
> *Ricardo.*—(*Pleased, to Don Florín*) Did you hear that? Remarkable! A good, old-fashioned ghost. (*To the Ghost*) Congratulations, my friend. What a splendid baritone voice to speak of the immortality of the soul! (*The Ghost sneezes and draws away from the window.*) Don't be afraid; this gentlemen is a friend. Won't you sit down?
> *Fantasma.*—Miserable mortal! . . . (*He sneezes twice in rapid succession and drops his tone.*) The window, please.

The entire scene with the Ghost—the contrast of the initial greeting, solemn and disdainful, with the subsequent sneezes, the switch from an unnatural to a natural tone of voice—is light and comic, mostly because of the contrast between the conventional idea of ghosts and the pathetic figure of Don Joaquín, the most natural of supernatural beings. He explains that when Ricardo arrived with obvious intentions to stay despite his spectral maneuvers, he found himself obliged to haunt the house seriously. To do so, he had to fortify his knowledge of methods. He began to read mystery stories, but succeeded only in frightening himself. Now he sees ominous shadows lurking everywhere, preying upon him; and yesterday, the house began to move, the walls closing in upon him. Ricardo and Florín explain that the reason for the extraordinary occurrence is simply that Don Joaquín has drunk a bottle of rum with his meal. His unghostlike reaction is, "Really? My word, what harm it does me. . . ."

Ricardo's reaction to Don Joaquín is also humorous, though somewhat brutal. He forces him, notwithstanding his timidity, to adopt Napoleon's lofty mannerisms. When Joaquín returns again to the stage, he is dressed to suit the part he is forced to play. His appearance interrupts a scene, quite intense and serious, between Ricardo and Sirena. The contrast between the two situations makes his appearance all the more ludicrous. His dialogue and actions are by their simplicity extremely humorous. He enters solemnly, as usual, his hand upon his breast in Napoleonic fashion:

Fantasma.—An astral greeting, human! The clock has struck twelve. Bong . . . Bong . . .

Ricardo.—(*Pushing him aside without looking at him*) Sirena! (*He exits following her.*)

Fantasma.—Well; tonight there is no performance. Good.

Pedrote enters at this point with Samy, who sits in reflexive silence. Joaquín decides that there is going to be a performance after all:

Fantasma.—. . . Soldiers, from the summit of those pyramids forty centuries contemplate your bravery!

Samy.—(*Naturally*) Good evening.

Fantasma.—I haven't made any effect. (*He draws closer.*) You probably think that you're talking with Napoleon, don't you? And that I died on an island, right? Yes, that's what they say. But actually my name is Don Joaquín. Just like it sounds. What do you think? Huh? (*Putting his hand on Samy's shoulder*) Say, friend.

Samy.—(*A mechanical, "jack-in-the-box" greeting*) Good evening. (*Back to his silence*)

Fantasma.—Now I get it! You're Mr. Samy. You can't imagine how anxiously Don Ricardo has awaited your arrival. I understood from him that you were a gay and impulsive fellow. All of us here are impulsive. All of us. My goodness, my goodness, you're Mr. Samy . . . I was anxious for your arrival, too. Don Ricardo says that you will teach me to make my reentry into mortality . . . Since he insists that I have already made my exit.[10] Peculiarities of his.

Fantasy versus Reality

> He is a great fellow, that Ricardo. Hm? (*Seeing that Samy is not paying the least attention to him*) Granite!
> *Ricardo.*—(*Serious*) Samy!
> *Samy.*—(*Getting up*) Ricardo!
> *Fantasma.*—Soldiers, from the summit of those pyramids . . .
> *Ricardo.*—Out! (*The Fantasma exits.*)

Many comic devices are used in this brief scene. The contrast of this scene with the preceding one, Joaquín's exaggerated simplicity, and his effusive attempts to engage Samy's attention in contrast to the latter's implacable silence form the greatest part of the humor of this situation. Joaquín's abrupt, mechanical adaptation of the Napoleonic pose at Ricardo's appearance also adds measurably to the comic effect.

Henri Bergson states what he considers to be a law of comedy: "Any arrangement of acts and events is comic which gives us, in a single combination, the illusion of life and the distinct impression of a mechanical arrangement."[11] No greater corroboration for this law could be found than the exaggerated calm with which the Pastor and the Illusionist in *Los árboles mueren de pie* converse while the Illusionist methodically and mechanically fills the stage with bizarre effects. As laughter seems to beget laughter, each new trick grows better than the last. A portion of their dialogue will illustrate the point:

> *Pastor.*—This is getting worse every day. If we weren't all idealists at heart!
> *Illusionist.*—I'll tell you. As far as I'm concerned, idealism . . . (*He collapses his cane on the floor and puts it in his pocket.*)
> *Pastor.*—Working much?
> *Illusionist.*—Not much. Old people, children, servants . . . Matinée! (*While looking for something, he takes out a flute, blows a chord on it and puts it in another pocket.*) And what about you? Happy?
> *Pastor.*—Out of my element. I was born for the university. (*Nostalgically*) The Sorbonne, Oxford, Bologna . . .
> *Illusionist.*—I was born for the circus: Hamburg, Marseille, Barcelona . . . (*Goes through the same motions with some handkerchiefs that change color as they slip through his hands*)

> *Pastor.*—Bookshelves to the ceiling, the school bell, the Gothic cloister . . .
>
> *Illusionist.*—The old canvas tent, the highways. . . . Look at what we have come to, my friend. Banana?
>
> *Pastor.*—No, thanks. (*The Illusionist peels and eats his philosophically.*)

As Casona advises in his stage directions, neither individual shows the slightest surprise at these puerile tricks. "They face each other with a doctoral tone and a resigned, plebeian lethargy."

Prohibido suicidarse en primavera suffers greater inconsistencies in characterization, greater abuse of coincidence, and certainly places greater emphasis on sentimentality than the other two plays. But Casona's humor again redeems these faults. Harry Allen Overstreet has said, "Humor brings the incongruous elements out into the open, sets them face to face with each other."[12] This sort of conflict often results from our attention being diverted from the moral, aesthetic, or emotional aspect of a situation to the physical. A comic effect is achieved, says Bergson, when the body takes precedence over the soul, ". . . the manner seeking to outdo the matter, the letter aiming at ousting the spirit." There is a sort of macabre comicality in the coldly businesslike manner in which Roda, Hans, Fernando, and sometimes Chole consider suicide. After the purpose of the Home has been explained to him, Fernando's reaction is, "Journalistically, it would be more interesting if they killed themselves," thus making suicide only a physical act calculated solely to satisfy a public hungry for unusual and morose human events. The answer to his next question is of similar complexion:

> *Fernando.*—. . . Haven't you ever run into the authentic suicide, the irretrievably hopeless case?
>
> *Doctor.*—Only those who are still hesitant come here. Unfortunately, those who are completely hopeless kill themselves anywhere, without the least respect for technique or for Dr. Ariel.

The simple Hans, a "mutilated soul," is especially prone to emphasize the physical to the exclusion of the moral or emotional. The Imaginary Lover finally becomes exasperated with this tendency:

Doctor.—Have you chosen your . . . method?
Lover.—No, not yet. I was thinking about it.
Hans.—(*Offering the merchandise like items in a bazaar*) We have a special willow tree for lovers, a legendary lake . . . If you like the classics, we can offer you a bouquet of roses with an asp, Cleopatra style, a warm bath, Socratic hemlock . . .
Lover.—Why so many? When life gets unbearable, any old tree will do.
Hans.—(*Hastening to make note in his notebook*) Ah, very good . . . "Suspension." Perfect. Neck size?
Lover.—Thirty-seven, long.
Hans.—Thirty-seven. Do you have a preference for a particular kind of tree?
Lover.—(*Reacting suddenly*) Oh, shut up, I can't listen to you. You have the coldness of a public official. It's revolting to hear you talk like that about death.

A partial repetition of this scene makes it twice as humorous; Doctor Roda has obtained a pledge from Fernando and Chole that they will aid him in his responsibilities, which they proceed to do as follows:

Fernando.—Have you chosen your method?
Chole.—Don't decide without consulting with us. We have the best poisons, a legendary lake, individual cells and . . .
Lover.—(*Suddenly*) You, too! Shut up! Everything is cold here . . . hatefully cold. I expected to find a companion spirit.

It is, in fact, a stress upon physical or mechanical aspects of life and death that causes a further breakdown in the Dama Triste's (Sorrowful Lady's) resolve to destroy herself. She confides to Fernando that she would like to die for love, but (alas!) that requires two willing hearts. Would Fernando care to . . . ? Ah, no. Unfortunately, he has given his word to another—he has promised he would kill himself with a Polish pianist. The poor Dama always arrives too late. But how she has dreamed of dying with her lover, as Japanese lovers sometimes do, hand in hand as they throw themselves into the depths of the crater Fuji-Yama! Fernando is sympathetic: "A beautiful way to go," he says. "Unfortunately, Spain is a degenerate country. We haven't even one miserable volcano left for such cases." The Dama sighs disconsolately. Fernando continues the conversation and discovers that she wishes to die because she feels alienated from this materialistic world; her flesh has never lived. Only her soul. He questions her about her habits—what she eats, if she has traveled, if she has ever loved, if she likes to read, finally revealing the startling facts of an extraordinary discovery!

> *Fernando.*—(*Who has been taking notes and adding numbers rapidly*) Splendid. Now, then, Madam: If we figure only half your life, and modest portions of everything, the results are: in order to make three short voyages, learn to play the piano, read the works of Victor Hugo and kiss a naval lieutenant . . . you would have to have consumed two thousand one hundred and twelve gallons of milk, three wagonloads of fruit, twenty acres of peas, and seventeen calves! The body, Madam, is an insubornable reality!
> *Dama.*—(*Horrified*) No! It's not possible!
> *Fernando.*—Mathematically exact.
> *Dama.*—How shameful.

In the same play, Hans, in his simplicity, mistakes the form for the spirit of the occasion when he complains about the Philosophy Professor's falling in love with the Dama Triste:

> *Fernando.*—Has that woman gone crazy?
> *Hans.*—Worse than that. Haven't you heard her humming "The Blue Danube"?
> *Fernando.*—That's what it sounded like.
> *Hans.*—Doesn't that remind you of anything?
> *Fernando.*—The Professor of Philosophy!
> *Hans.*—None other. Last night I caught them together in the moonlight, among the acacias. (*Philosophically*) Have you ever noticed what cows' eyes look like?
> *Fernando.*—Yes. They are the image of humid tenderness.
> *Hans.*—Well: last night the Professor of Philosophy had cows' eyes. They were sitting on a bank. He was looking at

Fantasy versus Reality 95

        the moon. Then he'd look at her. And then he'd sigh. When a professor of philosophy dares to sigh, he's lost.

Fernando.—Did you see them?

   Hans.—What haven't I seen in my lifetime? They were very close together, holding hands. He leaned his head over her shoulder, and murmured something slow and intimate in her ear.

Fernando.—Poetry?

   Hans.—Probably. I couldn't catch more than a verse or so. It went like this: (*Reciting lyrically*) "Any body submersed in water loses a quantity of weight equal to the weight of the liquid it displaces." Just imagine!

Casona's sense of irony is evident in the situation where Cora Yako, in her pursuit of the hapless Lover, makes a rather grave miscalculation:

   Cora.—. . . I got up singing, I went all around these mountains shouting your name, and I took a bath in the stream. Since then I've been throwing rocks at your window. Were you sleeping so soundly?

   Lover.—But I've been up since dawn.

   Cora.—And you didn't hear me? I threw rocks at first, until I broke the windows, then I threw bouquets of violets. Didn't you even get the violets?

We learn later of the extent of her error. The circumspect Hans received the flowers!

   Hans.—That Cora Yako has finally succeeded in driving me out of my mind. It's insulting! . . .

Fernando.—She has a lot of life, that one.

   Hans.—Too much. (*Confidential*) Did you know she tried to seduce me?

Fernando.—You!

   Hans.—Me! This morning. I was shaving quietly at the window and, playfully almost, she began to throw rocks at me. I had to take cover inside. She threw four rocks the size of pecans through the windows. And then, a bouquet of violets. I can take the rocks, but a bouquet of violets . . . ! There are things a lady does *not* do, Madam!

There are many other avenues to explore relative to Casona's place in the currents of thought in our century; indeed, many articles have already been written that investigate other phases of his works. Charles Leighton, the most active of Casona's critics, has summarized his point of view concerning the playwright in our era in an article entitled "Alejandro Casona y las ideas," wherein he exposes Casona's relationship to such modern phenomena as existentialism, Freud, Pirandello, Lorca, Erich Fromm, and others.[13]

We have traced Casona's place on the solipsistic scale, touching upon his sense of dramatic structure and his sense of humor. For the curious reader who would probe other questions, it may be suggested that Casona's thematic choice reminds one of Giraudoux, as does his sense of equilibrium in blending the serious with the comic. His antipositivistic bent and the types of humor he follows recall Henri Bergson.[14] Despite certain critics' allegations to the contrary, Casona holds a firm place in the mainstream of twentieth-century thought and letters.[15]

Chapter Four
The Paranormal

Casona cannot accept that anyone, scientist, laborer, or priest, can argue away the miracle of life. His preoccupation with the spiritual side of man and his rejection of strict materialism have led him often to venture into the "twilight" areas of human thought and behavior—the areas termed "paranormal." It is, of course, impossible to determine the extent to which he personally believed in, for example, extrasensory perception (ESP), but it seems safe to assume that he did not reject its possible validity. His plea for a more imaginative world and his insistence upon individual worth as opposed to institutionalism readily explain such an attitude. He confesses an interest, if not a belief, in such phenomena in his essay "Saudades," wherein he tells of a *déjà vu* experience:

I went predisposed to find something familiar, but what I could not imagine is that upon seeing Lisbon for the first time, I would "recognize" it suddenly, as though I had lived there in some forgotten time. This curious phenomenon before an unknown place has surprised all of us at some time or another: "I have been here before!" Magic anticipation? Superimposure of fantasy and reality, as in those lightning-dreams that we dream at the precise moment of awakening? A former life? (Are there souls with pages torn out as in old books . . . ?) I don't know. Priestly has written a suggestive comedy about that. The fact of the matter is that I "already knew," I don't know how or when, that Lisbon spread out like Rome over seven hills, that Moorish section of La Alfama, that Hell's Maw of Cascaes, that misty green of the Sintra Mountains. I had not memorized a single one of Camoens's verses, and yet, upon arriving on an afternoon of blustery swells at the Cabo de Roca . . . , the farewell of "Os Lusiadas" came up in my throat with the most astonishing naturalness: "Here the land ends . . . and the sea begins."[1]

Some form of ESP is suggested in the majority of Casona's plays. In *Las tres perfectas casadas* (The three perfect wives) Ada has *corazonadas* ("presentiments"); Estela in *La barca sin pescador* (*Boat Without a Fisherman*) senses that there is "something dark" between her and Ricardo; Pablo in *La tercera palabra* (The third word) senses the presence of death, God, and spring; Podgers's chiromancy in *El crimen de Lord Arturo* (Lord Arthur's crime), a dramatization of Oscar Wilde's story, likewise presents an interesting example of precognition or clairvoyance.

In this chapter we shall consider the three plays that concede a preeminent role to the paranormal, *Siete gritos en el mar* (Seven cries at sea), *La llave en el desván* (Key in the attic), and *La casa de los siete balcones* (The house of the seven gables). The treatment, deviating slightly from the format so far established, first presents a plot summary of each play, and then conclusions are drawn that summarize my critical reaction to all three plays.

Siete gritos en el mar (Seven cries at sea)

This play deals with a remarkable dream by a reporter, Juan de Santillana. Casona himself explains the dream's origin:

Upon reading many things about dreams (Freud, Adler, Jung, etc.) in order to write *La llave en el desván* (the work that immediately preceded *Siete gritos en el mar*), I discovered something very simple that had always seemed mysterious to me; the fact that we dream a story of shipwreck and when we awaken we find that the water is running in the bathroom; or [we dream] that someone is strangling us, and when we awaken the pillow is pressed against our throat. We think that the "end of a long dreamed story" coincides "with an immediate reality." The explanation is, of course, the opposite: the pillow causes us to dream the entire story that leads to the assassin who is strangling us, because the dream in its entirety lasts a thousandth of a second.

The table next to Santillana (in *Siete gritos en el mar*) falls; as it strikes the floor, it suggests a detonation, and Santillana puts into electric circulation all his preoccupations (peace and war, the mystery of Nina, the suggestion of Julia—with whom, as the dream reveals to him, he has fallen in love—etc., etc.). And when the Steward approaches to lift the table back up and awaken him, the whole play has taken place.[2]

The dream was precipitated by the sound of the falling table, but evoked by an old sea captain's memoirs. The action unfolds on board the passenger ship *Nalón*. It is Christmas Eve, and the Captain has invited Santillana and seven other guests to dine with him. They include Julia Miranda, whose "sin" is that she has lost all hope; Nina, who in reality is not married to Baron Pertus but who for some time has been masquerading as his wife; the Baron; Santiago Zabala, who caused the death of his first wife, not directly, but by the subtle cruelty of wishing her dead so he could marry Mercedes (his first wife finally committed suicide); Mercedes Zabala, now married to Santiago but carrying on an affair with Harrison; Harrison, manufacturer of arms and a traitor to all humanity; and the Professor of Irony (*profesor de ironía*), whose cynicism has eroded away the hopes of so many of his students.

Santillana has fallen asleep while reading the Captain's memoirs and awakens, apparently, while the Captain and the Steward are preparing for the evening's festivities. The Captain graciously gives Santillana permission to go on reading, but, preferring to reserve the last page for himself, he tears it from the book. When all the guests are assembled, the Captain tells them that his ship is to act as a decoy for enemy submarines. His country is at war, and they are members of a suicide mission. The guests cannot at first believe that the Captain is serious, but as the time draws nearer, they see that he is indeed in earnest. The Captain predicts that they all will, each in his own way, utter "a cry at sea." He hints at the sham and hypocrisy of each individual, disclosing his unusual perception. And, as predicted, one by one they end up either confessing their sins to ease their conscience at the threat of death, or, in the case of Harrison, fleeing in cowardice. Harrison, the most despicable of all, is shot in his attempt to escape. When the time comes for the attack, the explosion occurs in the midst of total darkness, following which the opening scene is repeated, this time with a new young Captain who is expecting the illustrious guests already seen. The whole play has been the reporter's dream, a strange dream wherein the lives of his fellow passengers have been revealed to him as they really are.

La llave en el desván (The key in the attic)

Mario, the protagonist, is a brooding, neurotic engineer whose hopes for professional and financial success crumble at the news that a large American firm has anticipated him by producing the same type of industrial furnace he has been years developing. Everyone but Laura (his sister-in-law, who has come to act as his nurse) believes that this economic and moral setback is the cause of the severe emotional upheaval he suffers. She is convinced that the nightmares and anxiety that beset him have deeper causes. The old family doctor and friend, Don Gabriel Miranda, comes to share Laura's point of view after witnessing the aftermath of a very disturbing dream Mario has had. Laura and Gabriel are discussing Mario's situation when they hear a shot in the direction of the garden. They conclude that it is Anselmo, the gardener, shooting at martins, but Mario enters with the alarming report that he has just killed his wife, Susana. Laura runs to the garden but finds nothing. It has been a nightmare, which Mario relates in detail once they have finally succeeded in calming him. He had been reading in the pavillion house when he fell asleep. The dream began, he explains, in a storm. He suddenly had the sensation of danger—a dog was barking, and the barking grew louder and came nearer. He took the shotgun from the wall, and suddenly, at the door of the pavillion, under three white poplar trees, the dog appeared, threatening, looking at him through wild, copper-colored eyes. This was the only color in the dream; all other images were in black and white.

Mario raised his gun to fire, but at that instant a veiled woman carrying a riding crop and wearing a riding habit with a lace collar thrust herself between him and the rabid beast, protecting it with her person. He could not refrain from pulling the trigger, and the woman fell dead. Though he did not see her face, and though there was nothing about her he could immediately associate with her, he is certain the woman was his wife. Everything took place while the tower clock chimed three.

Mario tries to dismiss the whole matter as unimportant. There have never been dogs on the place, there are no three white poplars, and Susana is very much alive. What significance can the dream possibly have? But Gabriel is sure they have hit upon the beginning of something momentous. The fact that the woman in Mario's dream was veiled leads him to suspect that it was *not* Susana, despite Mario's insistence. Gabriel and Laura are divided in their opinions concerning the interpretation of the dream. Gabriel seeks the answer in Mario's past; Laura believes it is to be interpreted on the basis of present circumstances. She discovers a number of "cur"-like qualities that identify Alfredo, Mario's "friend" and partner, with the mad dog in his dream. It was Alfredo who stole the formula for Mario's project and sold it to the American firm; moreover, he has established a liaison with Susana, Mario's wife and Laura's sister. And most important, he has copper-colored eyes. But Don Gabriel uncovers certain factors that seem even more significant. In an old family album, he finds a photograph of Mario's mother carrying a riding crop and wearing a riding habit with a lace collar. He and Laura are both momentarily convinced that the figure from Mario's dream is his mother. Don Gabriel also finds an old sheet of music, the score for a melody Mario used to hear as a child, a melody that figured in one of his dreams. Gabriel calls in old Anselmo, who discloses that the mad dog in the dream had a counterpart in real life, as did the poplars that stood at the door of the pavillion house. The dog was a favorite pet Anselmo had to dispatch when it contracted rabies. He explains: "I put the gun to my shoulder three times, and I couldn't shoot. Finally, I clenched my teeth . . . , and pulled the trigger. That was when I heard that scream that still echoes. It was the child (Mario) who had seen everything, hidden among the poplars."

Mario relates two other dreams wherein he is bereft of his own identity and all his possessions. There is a clock that chimes three in one of them; the number three appears obsessively in all his dreams. Laura is almost convinced that Gabriel is correct in interpreting the dreams on the basis of past events, notwithstanding her belief that she has established a parallel between the mad dog and Alfredo. Not only do the dog and the three poplars have counterparts in Mario's painful repressions, but he confesses also that he witnessed his mother's death, which his dream has simulated through his identification with his father. While still a child, he heard a shot and ran to the window, and saw his father, shotgun in hand, standing over the inert form of his mother, a red spot on the lace collar of her riding habit. Then he saw his father leap on his horse and ride away. He rode for hour after purposeless hour, until they brought back his broken body following an accident, precipitated, apparently, by the skittish mount. But Mario has never been certain that it was an accident. He asks: "Was it the horse? Or was it the rider that forced them both over the bank? And if it was the rider, why? Why? My whole life as a man is nailed to that childhood question."

As it happens, both Laura and Gabriel are right. Gabriel, seeking the interpretation in the past, uncovers the story of Mario's father, who was faced with his wife's infidelity. Laura, seeking the interpretation in the present, comes to realize that history is repeating itself. Rain, thunder, and wind appear in the final scene as predictive symbols of an impending tragedy, a tragedy that has been enacted a generation earlier. Mario, during the storm, surprises Susana and Alfredo in their attempt to flee together, and shoots them both as the clock chimes three.

La casa de los siete balcones (The house of the seven gables)

The scene is the "house of seven gables," a manor house belonging to the Altamira family, all dead now except Genoveva, a forty-year-old spinster, and Uriel, son of Ramón and Genoveva's sister, whom Ramón married, thereby obtaining the bulk of the Altamira fortune. Ramón has squandered the wealth his marriage brought him, establishing a liaison with Amanda, the housekeeper (*ama de llaves*), a physically attractive, sensual, and extremely ambitious woman. Ramón's relations with Amanda, one chapter in a long history of infidelity, have alienated him from his son and from Genoveva. Moreover, Uriel is mute, and communicates only with Genoveva through a strange telepathic process that puzzles everyone. Genoveva still nurtures the hope that her fiancé, who left for America years ago, will send for her to join him. The truth is, he has long since married someone else, and Genoveva's fierce insistence, and her refusal to face the fact, causes everyone to believe she is mad.

Genoveva withholds from Ramón the secret of what remains of the hidden family fortune, which Ramón needs to liquidate gambling debts and pay for other profligacies. At one point, exasperated at Genoveva's refusal to yield her secret, Ramón throws her to the floor and threatens further injury to her when Uriel seizes an iron. Shouting "No," the word Genoveva has tried hardest to teach him, he protects his aunt against his bewildered father. Don Germán, a doctor and long-standing friend of the Altamiras, continues regularly to visit Genoveva and Uriel and defend Genoveva against Ramón's outbursts. In fact, he promises Ramón that he will kill him if ever he should separate Genoveva from Uriel, and warns him that that, precisely, is what Amanda is about. And indeed she is. She yearns to become the "señora" of the household, and obtains Ramón's promise that if she can extract Genoveva's secret from her he will have her committed to an asylum.

Amanda's plan succeeds. She falsifies a letter to Genoveva from her betrothed in America. Genoveva, finally convinced, is delirious with joy and does not hesitate to reveal where the fortune is hidden. They tell her they will take her to the boat that will carry her to America, but the intent is to have her committed this very night. Rosina, an innocent servant girl, goes to Uriel when she discovers the plot, and because she cares for him, she is somehow able to get across to him what is going on. He shouts "No" again, and rushes out to find Don Germán. With spurs buckled to his boots, he mounts a wild young horse and rides recklessly in the direction Don Germán has taken. Three other characters who have visited Uriel from time to time enter to await the outcome of this savage ride. They are Uriel's mother, his grandfather, and his childhood playmate, Alicia, who have been wont to appear to Uriel from the other side of death in his moments of greatest anguish. They do not wait long. There is a sound of hoofbeats offstage, then the sudden sharpness of an impact. Uriel joins them shortly, dressed, as they are, in spotless white. And Genoveva descends the stairs, ecstatically anticipating her journey to America!

Summary

In all three of these plays, one aspect of Casona's thought stands out: life is a beautiful mystery, a miracle scarcely to be circumscribed by the limitations of science. In *La llave en el desván,* Don Gabriel, with all his knowledge, respects the opinions, albeit superstitious ones, of those who believe in the annunciatory qualities of dreams. And Laura's analysis of Mario's dreams is, after all, just as valid as Don Gabriel's, while Santillana's dream in *Siete gritos en el mar* reveals the secret lives of his fellow passengers. Uriel in *La casa de los siete balcones* does receive visits from the dead, and hear Genoveva's voice, though all other voices fall short of his hearing. Love, itself a miracle, is a language that goes far beyond the limitations of ordinary language. When Don Germán in *La casa de los siete balcones* suggests as much to Rosina, she quotes a man "who has studied" as saying that there is no such thing as a miracle. Don German answers, "He probably hasn't studied long enough."

Always, beyond taxes, salaries, furs, and gadgets, beyond all the discoveries of science, there lies a country whose mysteries have never been fully explored, and whose borders few dare to cross. Casona dares. And he has discovered the miracle that is love, the miracle that is death, the miracle that is God. Love is a way of communicating. There may be many other ways. Casona would not reject the possible validity of ESP.

Chapter Five
Historical Plays

Though Casona's plays are, for the greater part, set in the present day, it is not surprising, considering his strong feeling for the past, that he should on occasion turn toward history for his dramatic material. Three of his plays deal with historic figures. One is a tender and passionate love story, one is based on the life of a great musician, and the last on the life of a great poet. These plays are *Corona de amor y muerte* (*Crown of Love and Death*), the story of Inés de Castro and Pedro, the crown prince of Portugal; *Sinfonía inacabada* (Unfinished symphony), a version of the Franz Schubert story; and *El caballero de las espuelas de oro* (The knight with the golden spurs), the story of Francisco de Quevedo. We shall consider here two of the three plays, the first and the last.

Corona de amor y muerte (*Crown of Love and Death*)

A summary of Casona's version of the Inés de Castro tale is as follows:

In the first scene the Princess Constanza arrives with her retinue at Coimbra; Maestre is proclaiming the schedule of festive events that will celebrate her arrival. Bells are ringing, the houses are draped in white—even the white splendor of the trees in blossom seems to commemorate the occasion. The Infanta and Pedro, the crown prince, are to be married. But Constanza is not attentive. Something troubles her. We soon learn that the marriage is considered a royal duty, that Pedro is already in love with and living with another woman—a situation Constanza has previously suspected.

The second scene shows Pedro and Ines together. Their home is a domestic haven, with three children and a nurse, Amarantha, who is married to Fragoso, Pedro's servant and hunting companion. Aware of the exigencies of the Prince's position, Inés and Pedro realize that he must go to the palace to face the situation awaiting him there. In the third scene, Pedro and the King, who wills the marriage, come together. Pedro, intransigent, refuses to give up Inés; the King, equally intransigent, insists that his son comply with his orders. Maestre introduces the Infanta, and the King retires with the tacit threat of reprisal should Pedro not accede to the royal demand. But Pedro, alone with Constanza, tells her that his loyalties to Inés are firm. She, with equal calm, informs him that she cannot suffer the indignity of having come all the way to Portugal to be spurned. They take leave of each other almost amiably.

The second act is set in Inés's home. Constanza, in order to distract the rest of the group, has arranged with one of her ladies-in-waiting to have a convenient "accident" while on the King's hunting party. She, in the meantime, consumed with curiosity, goes to meet Inés. Though by her own affirmation she finds nothing extraordinary about her rival, she cannot intimidate her; the Infanta of Castille is humbled by Inés's serenity in the face of dire threats. Inés will suffer anything for Pedro. Before the Infanta leaves, another surprise visitor comes, for the first time, to Inés's household—it is King Alfonso, Pedro's father. Constanza leaves, and the King, alone with Inés, importunes her strongly to leave Pedro, but she refuses. The King, notwithstanding his astonishment at her quiet strength and firmness, makes it very clear that he will keep his word to Castille at all costs. At this point Juan, Inés's oldest son, enters. Inés manages to leave Alfonso alone with his grandson, for whom he shows a great deal of tenderness and seems about to be won over when Pedro enters. Juan is made to leave, and the inevitable argument between Alfonso and Pedro ensues. Pedro tells his father that he and Inés are legitimately married. Thereupon, the King hardens once more and leaves the house with the ominousness of his royal threat still echoing behind him.

Pedro's meeting with his father in the final act represents a stronger clash of personalities than ever; Pedro learns that a sentence of death threatens Inés, but he is taken prisoner and can do nothing to help her. In the second scene, the King goes with his counselors to Inés's house to carry out the sentence they have passed. The King urgently pleads with Inés to leave and escape the consequences of her union with Pedro, but she prefers death to a life of separation from him. The curtain falls as the King's counselors are approaching to perform the execution. Inés appears to Pedro as an ethereal figure in the final scene. After she leaves, Fragoso runs in to announce her death. Pedro, then, makes an impassioned plea to his men, summoning them to rally against his father. The stage darkens amid the din of battle, then all is quiet except for the music of a mournful rebec, which dissolves into sacred organ music. The light comes up slowly on the coronation scene, wherein Pedro crowns the ethereal figure of Inés Queen of Portugal.

The Historical Incident[1]

Notwithstanding the legend-makers' sometimes complicated embellishments, the actual story of Inés de Castro is a simple one. In measurably reduced terms, it is this:[2] Inés was born near the beginning of the fourteenth century, the illegitimate daughter of Pedro Fernández de Castro, lord of Galicia, and Doña Aldonza Soares de Valladares. She was educated in the palace of Don Juan Manuel, author of *El conde Lucanor*. In 1340, Juan Manuel's daughter Constanza journeyed to the Portuguese court in Coimbra to marry Pedro, the crown prince. Unions between the Portuguese and Castilian royalty were common in this time of uneasy peace, and the marriage had actually been performed by proxy four years earlier. Constanza's distant cousin, Inés de Castro, was a member of her retinue. Pedro married Constanza, but fell in love with Inés. The king, in a vain effort to stop Pedro from seeing Inés, immediately banished her to the castle of Albuquerque on the border of Estremadura.

At twenty-one, Constanza died following the birth of their third child. Thereupon, Pedro brought Inés back to the castle at Coimbra to live with him, and they also had three children: Joao (Juan), Dionís, and Beatriz. Pedro wanted the line of succession to continue through Inés's son Juan. After a long but ultimately successful uprising against Pedro's father, Inés met a tragic death at the hands of the king's followers; Portuguese legend claims that Pedro held a posthumous coronation and declared Inés Queen of Portugal.

In his introduction to the play, Casona refers to it as "version forty-five"; he states that Antero de Figueiredo has counted forty-four dramatic versions of the Pedro-Inés-Constanza story. The most important drama on this subject before Casona's (Lope de Vega's has been lost) is that of Luis Vélez de Guevara (1578–1645). Both authors had access to the same poetry, history, and Portuguese legends; but the works are quite different. There is, first, the difference in language. Vélez's high-toned verses contrast measurably with Casona's dignified but very flexible prose. This is not to suggest that Casona's use of language is superior, but merely that he accedes to the demands of modern conventions. The audiences in Vélez's period expected the somewhat stiff verse dialogue. They expected the authors to be schooled in rhetoric and the actors in declamation. Casona's dialogue moves along at the pace of a lively repartee. Some of the characters' speeches in Vélez's play are on occasion as long as six pages; consequently, the scenes containing these speeches move very slowly. But the audience expected, and indeed demanded, passages long enough to provide an outlet for the actor's ability to declaim.

Modern conventions have placed greater strictures upon playwrights' representation of a character's thoughts. The aside, common in the theater just a few years ago, is rarely, if at all, allowed today. The soliloquy likewise is used rarely. Vélez uses both freely. Casona's play is shaped, to some measure, by convention, for he avoids elements that would be offensive to his audience. Coello and Alvargonzález, two advisors to the King who are ultimately involved in the murder of Inés, appear in Guevara's play as well as in Casona's. But Casona adds Pacheco, who in addition to being one of the King's counselors is a close friend of Pedro and appears to be almost in love with Inés. This change gives additional pathos to the final scenes, and when Pacheco finally agrees that Inés must be killed, the decision has even greater validity as a political necessity. Although Casona alters some of the major historical facts, he displays his historical awareness and comprehensive reading by his accuracy in many minor points. At the beginning of the last scene of the play, Pedro hears a shepherd playing his rebec and remarks, "That discordant music irritates me." The historical Pedro, according to the chronicles of Fernán López, insisted upon trumpet music even at dances, and "if at any time they wanted to play stringed instruments, he soon grew irritated and told them to give them to the Devil and call the trumpeters."[3]

It is in his handling of Constanza's arrival and Pedro's relationship to Inés that Casona takes the greatest liberties with historical reality. In their introduction to the play, Balseiro and Owre comment on Casona's "fortunate anachronism" of having Inés and Constanza arrive at the palace separately—years apart, in fact (xvii). By the time Constanza arrives, Inés has already established herself as Pedro's mistress and has borne him three children; she can therefore more easily serve a literary purpose as a representation of true love, in opposition to Constanza as the choice of the palace. Balseiro and Owre claim that Pedro's marriage to Constanza and the testaments of the time make it unlikely that Pedro could have been secretly married to Inés. But they add, "Historians are uncertain whether Pedro and Inés were ever married. Casona seems to know his heroine so well, his portrait of her is so sure, so intimate and human, that he leaves his readers not the slightest doubt but that she and Pedro were man and wife" (xvi).

Dramatic Techniques

Because the play is not particularly complex in its construction and because the conflict is quite simple, the exposition is not extensive. Before half of the first scene is over, we have learned that Constanza has come to marry Pedro, that the marriage is considered a royal duty, that Pedro is already in love with and living with another woman, and that Constanza suspects he has a mistress. So subtly is this information presented that it does not really occur to us to question how it is possible for Constanza to learn upon arrival of things that Maestre and her own ladies-in-waiting are careful to keep from her. Indeed, our awareness of Pedro's situation does not develop out of the relationship between any of the characters on stage. Casona uses a trick to bring the information to his audience. He introduces a group we never see, a band of students (traditional trouble makers) who harass the Princess and her retinue with a song that summarizes previous events. But Maestre interrupts the singers before they can finish the song and the Infanta is left with her curiosity. She will not be satisfied until she learns how the song ends. It is her insistence that brings about the rest of the exposition.

Besides carrying the exposition, which gives background facts and reveals the relationship of characters toward each other, the first scene shows Constanza sensing her predicament. The second deals, perhaps a little more sympathetically, with Pedro and Inés, whose relationship is the obstacle to Constanza's marriage. The third scene brings the sides together. Pedro tells his father he will not agree to marry Constanza. Then, face to face with Constanza, he repeats his intent to remain faithful to Inés; Constanza, with equal dignity, clarity, and firmness, informs him that she has no intention of compromising *her* position. There is very little action in the first act following the first half of the first scene, and this lack of action actually contributes to the rising tension of the drama, for we realize that the strong wills of the King, Pedro, and Constanza have caused a stalemate.

The second act, which takes place in Inés's home, brings Constanza and Inés together. Notwithstanding the fact that Constanza's pride is broken when she realizes Inés's strength and the great love she has for Pedro, and notwithstanding the King's tenderness toward his grandchild, nothing has really changed. The two sides are as uncompromising as ever. Casona brings us to the point of almost solving the problem, then backs away, allowing the sides to regroup and strengthen their positions for the final offensive. The second act represents, as it were, the "lull before the storm." The tension begins to rise again in the third act when Pedro and the King meet once more as they did in act 1. The near capitulation of the King in act 2 seems now to have steeled him against any further flexibility, for he clashes with his son more forcefully than before; there are threats and ultimatums on both sides. From here on, the various scenes in the play move the action swiftly toward the inevitable solution. The King, acting out of political necessity, orders Inés's death; Pedro, acting out of a total romantic commitment to Inés, declares war against his father. After a stage blackout symbolizing the long battle, we see the victorious Pedro crowning Inés Queen of Portugal in a posthumous ceremony.

Practically everything in act 1 prefigures something that develops later. Constanza admits that she is given to an almost unnatural curiosity, and this is evident in her reaction to the students' song. Having heard her admission and seen her react as a curious person once, one is not surprised to see her do so again in the second act, when she cannot refrain from visiting Inés. In the second scene of act 1, Casona presages events to come by means of a symbolic reference. This scene, in which Pedro and Fragoso discuss the relative merits of various types of hunting hawks, serves one purpose in showing Pedro as the virile and energetic hero; a second purpose becomes clear when the parallel emerges between Pedro's description of the ferocious and efficient but basically cowardly African hawks whose only method of attack is treachery and the actions of his father and his friend Pacheco when they sentence Inés to death. The second act opens with a similar dialogue between Pedro and Fragoso, but this time their discussion turns upon the matter of cowardly hunters who use gunpowder or crossbows and leave the game no defense. The helpless animal again parallels Inés's situation, for she has no recourse against the physical and legal power of the King and his followers.

From the time Inés speaks her first lines, she conveys in many different ways her feeling that her tragic end is imminent. She has *saudade,* a great longing, for everything she cannot touch or see, and Pedro chides her when she expresses her constant fear that their happiness is too great to endure. Another indication of her approaching death appears in the third scene of the first act when the King asks Pedro what sacrifice Inés would be willing to make for him and he answers, "She would go to her death with her eyes closed." The entire third act builds to that conclusion, which comes as no surprise. The King states, "When a knot cannot be untied, it must be cut," preparing spectators for Inés's death, as obviously he feels he has no alternative but to sentence her.

Earlier reference was made to the number of details that accumulate in the first scene to accomplish the exposition and introduce the conflict. This concentration of details is, of course, closely related to Casona's handling of motivation and use of foreshadowing. Another of Casona's methods of concentration is his use of a fairly small number of characters. Fragoso, Pedro's hunting companion, also brings the news of Inés's death; Elvira, Constanza's lady-in-waiting, becomes a more important character when Constanza asks her to distract the hunting party so that she can visit Inés; Amaranta fills the roles of servant, lady-in-waiting, and nurse in the household of Inés and Pedro; and the Maestre, who reads the proclamation of the wedding celebration in the first act, finishes the play by reading the coronation proclamation.

Obviously, the dramatic form imposes certain limitations upon the author, for he cannot describe his characters directly or specifically analyze their motives. Information is conveyed about them fundamentally through their own actions and through other characters' reactions to them. But there are other subtle ways that may substitute for the fictional author's summary. In the first scene, Constanza's actions are leading, for notwithstanding the festive atmosphere and the glowing description of events in Maestre's report, her thoughts are elsewhere. When she explains her troubles, it is with restraint and dignity, but with a certain incisiveness that indicates that such firmness and dignity are characteristic. Moreover, Casona has her give a self-analysis when she says, ". . . Neither Castille nor I knows how to wait!" Such analysis does not seem contrived because the conversation between her and the King justifies her reaction. The Prince, who should be there to welcome her, has not appeared. The King's reaction is another self-analysis: "I have always approved of those who dare to do the same as I would have done." It too is justified, for he is bound, under the circumstances, not to offend the Infanta, but he must at the same time maintain his own position; he chooses words that will not compromise his dignity, yet they make him and the Infanta allies, while also constituting a tacit revelation of his own pride and sense of fairness. King Alfonso is clearly neither hard-hearted nor vindictive. Casona shows him later reacting tenderly toward his grandson, and still later shows his overwhelming reluctance to sentence Inés.

When, in the second scene, Pedro appears, the public is prepared for his self-willed stance. The King has called him an "unbridled colt," with whom it became impossible to live any longer. Alvargonzález has accused him of extremes in his behavior; Coello also implies that his actions are something less than reasonable; and of course, his absence, under the circumstances, bespeaks a certain stubbornness. His strength and Inés's fragility are made visible as the two characters complement each other. Likewise, the personalities of the Infanta and Inés contrast with each other in the second act.

Authorial Ideology

Finally, we must answer the question, *why* has the author created such characters? It would be simpler if the audience were presented with a clear-cut case of good versus evil, but that would ruin the strength of the conflict. Casona allows Constanza the admiration her dignity can inspire in the first scene; he purposely shows the King to be a loving father, though he is unable to express the full extent of his feeling for his son Pedro or his tenderness toward his grandson. There is no idea, then, of an "enemy" or a good side and a bad one. In fact, if the figure of Pedro were not so compelling, sympathies would inevitably lie with the King. Rodríguez Richart remarks concerning Pedro: "Only that total passion and deep and devoted love could explain and justify dramatically the obstinate and rebellious attitude toward his father and toward the marriage that his father demands." The love scenes make clear that Pedro and Inés's deep feeling for each other is enough to cause them to place their own relationship above the commands of their King and the welfare of their nation. Casona's purpose, then, in creating the characters the way he does is to increase the poignancy of the conflict. The King's actions are politically inevitable and Pedro's are romantically inevitable, and both inspire sympathy; both are justified.

Another question that may occur to the careful reader, and one that indeed requires some attention, is why, in this play, set in fourteenth-century Portugal, and involving a highly emotional conflict and several moral questions, does Casona not present a single character who justifies his actions in religious terms, seeks the advice of a priest, or implores divine aid for his cause? Why does the playwright instruct specifically that the one real prayer in the play be recited "with the domestic simplicity of a daily occurrence"? Why does Inés, just before she is killed, choose to recite *Canción de amigo* (The lover's song) instead of a prayer? No doubt Casona wishes to allow all his characters' actions to evolve as logical reactions to the problems facing them; his characters are motivated by each other and their own bents and reservations, not by any outside force. To Inés, the *Canción de amigo* is a prayer; as far as she and Pedro are concerned, their love for each other is their ultimate surety and source of faith. It is this absolute and overwhelming love for each other, a humanistic faith transcending all else, that justifies them in their insistence upon continuing their relationship. For his part, the King claims at the close of the second act that he will not hesitate to declare illegal the marriage performed by Monseigneur Gil, that he will show him that ". . . within my borders there is only *one* authority. And that whatever Aviñón [the Pope] did yesterday can be undone today." The King is shown to lack religious feeling simply because it would be out of character as well as counterproductive for him to acknowledge any higher authority than himself.

The wellspring of a writer's art is a personal, characteristic attitude, which he will, in one way or another, almost inevitably reveal. Since the dramatist cannot communicate his feelings about a character or a situation through his own direct summary, the interpretation of the meaning he wishes to convey must be implicit—usually apparent through dramatic form (tragedy, comedy, melodrama, farce). Casona states that the theme of his play is "Love more powerful than death." The conflicts arising out of questions of love may obviously have universal significance; love represents one of humanity's insoluble problems. But it is the stature the author gives the conflict by treating it seriously—as a matter of life or death—that marks the work as possessing elements of tragedy and reveals his own attitude toward his subject. Love in its highest form is for Casona anything but commonplace. Sexual dalliance in no way parallels true love—in fact, love and sex are clearly distinct and separate. Leighton demonstrates this in his commentary on Casona's essay "Tres sonrisas de mujer" (Woman's three smiles), which sets forth the theory that whereas laughter and tears are spontaneous, primitive physiological manifestations, the smile must be cultivated and learned.[4] Casona envisions a clear parallel between laughter, tears, and sex on the one hand and the smile and love on the other. "Laughter, tears, and sex," he says, "are wild fruits that grow spontaneously in a cave; love and smiles are cultivated flowers that need a home to grow in." He adds:

> A child cries spontaneously at birth, and shortly thereafter he begins to laugh, without anyone's having to teach him those physical gestures of joy and pain; but only when he has developed mentally does he

smile. Thus Chateaubriand . . . defines infancy as the "age without smiles." and Balzac, carrying the poetic intent even further, affirms that women do not know smiles in their plenitude until they are mothers.

If we concur with Chateaubriand, and at the same time admit as valid the biogenetic law which stipulates that the life of a child is only a reproduction in reduced format of humanity's infancy, in strict logic we must conclude that during the long centuries that this period lasted, mankind lived under the rule of laughter and tears without suspecting the existence of that flower of the spirit that we call the smile—the same dark period approximately that he lived under the exclusive rule of sex without suspecting the existence of love.[5]

Here in very explicit form is the distinction between love and sex which is a touchstone of Casona's whole theater and sets him apart from Lorca on the one hand and Freud on the other.[6]

Casona further states, in his essay "La casa del Amor" (The house of love), that "the passion of love is in no way a common phenomenon, nor does it happen easily, every day, nor is it within reach of just any willing soul. The great majority of those who think they are in love have barely taken the first steps. Only exceptional spirits, and in circumstances likewise exceptional, have arrived at the highest point."[7] Inés de Castro, as Casona portrays her, is just such an exceptional spirit, placed in exceptional circumstances, and capable of fulfilling all the requirements for attaining the unique love experience he describes. "It is not a question of adding up two lives, but of fusing them so intimately that they come to create a third life, new and superior. . . . If man and woman do not renounce their individual singularity, they will never attain the totality of love."[8]

I am indebted to Jerald R. Foster for pointing out to me a number of parallels between Casona's Inés and the situation of Christ at the time of his crucifixion.[9] He reasons that Christ's love for mankind gave him strength to face the grueling events on the cross. Inés's love for Pedro in particular and for mankind in general likewise strengthens her in her final ordeal. Christ referred often to his imminent end. Inés's *saudade* rings with the strong premonition of the brevity of her own life. When Christ retired to pray in the Garden of Gethsemane on the eve of his martyrdom, he left three of his disciples at the gate.

They slumbered while he prayed. In the meantime, Judas conspired to betray him. During scene 2 of the final act of *Corona de amor y muerte,* Inés too is praying in a symbolic Gethsemane. As she prays, her three children, disciples to her love and motherhood, sleep, while her enemies conspire against her. As Christ finished his prayer, his enemies approached, and he "said to the multitudes, are ye come out as against a thief with swords and staves for to take me?" Inés has a similar reaction when she addresses the King and his retinue: "You mean all the lances and swords, all the soldiers and horses, are just against me?" From the crowd of Jesus' accusers stepped Judas to betray his Lord—Judas, who professed love for the Master, had dined with him, walked with him. He had also just come from a traitorous meeting with the ruling council of the Jews. Similarly, from among Inés's accusers steps Pacheco, who has eaten at her table and drunk water from the hollow of her hands, and kissed her palm as he finished the last swallow. Pacheco, professing love, has pronounced the sentence of death but a few hours earlier. Inés shows that she is puzzled by his involvement in the bloody affair, but she readily forgives the others, her "enemies." Christ's reaction to Judas was one of grave disappointment, but he too forgave his tormentors, averring that they knew not what they were about.

The King hesitates to sentence Inés, and confesses that she is innocent of actual conspiracy. His situation parallels that of Pontius Pilate, who was unwilling to sentence Jesus, and likewise acknowledged his innocence. Disturbing dreams concerning Jesus led Pilate's wife to advise him to avoid all entanglements with him. The King too has been troubled with portentous dreams involving Inés's children. Like Pilate, he wishes to be free from the responsibility of the execution, and pleads with Inés to free him from her death. Then, just as Pilate washed his hands of the affair, attempting to place the blame on the Jews, Alfonso shifts the responsibility to his underlings: "My lords! I swear before God that I have done everything possible to save this woman. Now what remains is in your hands." Casona seems to believe that love is an absolute. There is only one real love, personified in Christ. Clearly, the whole purpose behind these parallels is to compare Inés's all-consuming passion with that absolute Love.

The perfect fusion of sensual and mystic love, so characteristic of Inés, a superior soul in exceptional circumstances, is incomprehensible to the uninitiated spirit—as incomprehensible as Santa Teresa's mysticism. Witness the Infanta's perplexity in the face of Inés's explanation:

Infanta.—Then this famous business of love is no more than simple blindness?
Inés.—Much more; it's another way of seeing. Imagine yourself united with him until you are no longer yourself. His coldness is the only cold you feel, his fever burns you. Your separation hurts you like a wound, and if they cut off his hand you feel that your own is bleeding.
Infanta.—Then it's a kind of madness?
Inés.—It's much more; it's another kind of sanity.
Infanta.—I don't understand. I grasp those words when they apply to the soul, but the other love . . .
Inés.—What other?
Infanta.—The books speak of the soul and the flesh as enemies.
Inés.—Throw away those books. In true love the body and the soul are one inseparable substance, made of clay and of God. (With her arms crossed and a distant look in her eyes) When Pedro embraces me, my whole soul gradually takes on the form of his body. And in the morning, when he leaves, I'm empty, just like the clothing the laundryman leaves on the banks of the river: with the warmth of his leaving, and the shape of his returning.
Infanta.—Do you realize what you're saying? Have you no modesty?
Inés.—You have that before. And after.
Infanta.—(Gets up thoughtfully) It's useless . . . I try to understand you, but it's another language, another world . . .

Mingled with the patently sensual aspects of Inés's love—which arouse the Infanta's protest—are clear resonances of mysticism. Thus the Infanta can affirm her understanding of Inés's description as it applies to the soul, but fails to grasp the full impact of love as it involves the flesh. Esperanza Gurza concludes that Casona, combining poetic expressions of carnal love and mystical expressions ("another way of seeing" and "another kind of sanity"), "has formulated in a masterful way the essence of the mystical experience on the plane of human love." She goes on to point out Santa Teresa's articulation of the concept of mystical union and the necessity of fusing one's own will with the divine will, and even merging the individual identity with that of the Lord to gain personal strength. Teresa's strength is "in the Lord" in the same way that Inés's strength is in Pedro:[10]

> *King.*—What mysterious hidden power do you have?
> *Inés.*—No power of mine. It's he, who is standing inside me.
> *King.*—I don't believe in witchcraft, but . . . when she left here, why was the Infanta a conquered woman? And why has my son lost his senses? Why do my people sing your name in every street? What is your power, Inés?
> *Inés.*—I have no power. This voice you hear is nothing more than an echo of Pedro; this body you see is nothing more than his shadow. . . . I am so much a part of him that if he couldn't stand on his feet, I would fall to the floor. This infinite weakness is what you call power.

The strength of the theme fades slightly with Casona's sensational if somewhat superfluous ending. All the lights go out and we hear the sounds of battle; then we see a brief but very lavish coronation ceremony, and Pedro places the crown of Portugal upon the head of Inés's corpse. Casona betrays his desire to incorporate the most famous part of the Inés de Castro legend—the posthumous coronation—into his work, but the play as it is constructed simply does not need it. This final scene manages to satisfy the audience that Pedro was victorious and tries to suggest that his love for Inés (as well as hers for him) is immortal, but actually their love has triumphed long before the battle begins. The ending is superfluous, not only because most of the audience would already know that Pedro had won the battle, but also because the theme of the play does not depend in any way upon the outcome of the battle. Nor do we need a coronation scene to reassure us that it was the inspiration of Inés that caused Pedro to wage war against his father and emerge victorious. A much subtler and more sensitive suggestion of the immortality of their love comes at the end of scene 2, act 3, and scene 3 of the same act. Facing her executioners, Inés says that she will offer one last prayer. Her "prayer" is a *Canción de amigo,* a traditional Galician-Portuguese ballad (*Cançao de amigo*), the subject of which is usually a maid's lament over the absence of her lover. Love, if it truly is love and not an imitation, is the same, whether it be love of God or love of man. The "carnal" aspect of Inés's love is present in the tradition of the *Canción;* the notion of the "mystical union" through the experience of love comes to us through the suggestion that it is to Inés a prayer, a type of communion with God. Inés dies with the ballad on her lips, the strains of a distant rebec providing a dissonant accompaniment.

When the next scene opens, the music of the rebec is still heard, closely linking this scene with the last. Pedro is resting on an old tree trunk after a long march. He complains that the doleful music troubles him. When Inés appears, her words are from another old ballad, the *Romance del "Palmero,"* which is like an echo of the *Canción de amigo.* The dialogue that follows mellows our sympathy for Inés in moving crescendo, and reaches a climax of tenderness in the last four plaintive lines of the ballad:

> Sus cabellos eran de oro,
> sus manos como el marfil;
> siete condes la lloraban,
> caballeros más de mil . . .
>
> (Golden was her shining hair,
> Her hands were ivory white;
> Seven nobles wept for her,
> And more than a thousand knights.)

Casona's use of the ballads not only carries Inés from life into legend and immortality, but tacitly effects the fusion of carnal and spiritual love. If "God is Love," as the Bible affirms, then this form of true love is, as Casona presents it, an experience with God, or "communion" with him.

El caballero de las espuelas de oro
(Knight with the golden spurs)

The play is divided into two *tiempos* ("periods") of four scenes each. The first period shows Quevedo, at the apex of his career as the confidant and agent of the powerful Duke of Osuna, returning from Italy. He denounces the festering corruption of the government and sets himself at odds with the prevailing intellects of the day. The second period shows the bitter results of his campaign. The opening scene is set in a tavern where a group of individuals, giving themselves the name of the "Brotherhood of Laughter," has gathered. This is roughly reminiscent of certain institutions common to the seventeenth century, that is, the academies, similar in purpose to the French *salons,* and organized to provide outlet for the discussion of topics involving poetry, morals, and science. The haughty Pacheco de Narvaez, swordsman and official royal fencing master, enters out of curiosity, having heard that, notwithstanding the shabby appearance of the place, the food is excellent. About the same time, a stranger asks for admission to the Brotherhood. It is Francisco de Quevedo, whom the Brotherhood gladly welcomes. His presence triggers a series of discussions concerning current affairs, political and literary. Quevedo speaks out against courtly manipulations, favoritism in politics, *culteranismo* with its principal exponent, Góngora, and finally he scoffs at the absurdity of Pacheco de Narváez's theory dealing with the "science" of fencing—a science so exact that victory over one's opponent was a mere question of having calculated the proper geometric angle of the body in relation to the sword, etc. Pacheco, infuriated, faces Quevedo with the fact that *he* is Pacheco de Narváez—a revelation that fails to intimidate Quevedo. In fact, the latter challenges Pacheco to prove his point with the sword. Pacheco refuses at first, but the Brotherhood goads him into a confrontation wherein Quevedo disarms him twice. The King's principal swordsman is spared further humiliation by the arrival of the police.

In the second scene, a bookseller seeks Quevedo's help to stem the tide of resentment that is building against a dear friend of his, Lope de Vega. So bitter has the resentment become that it threatens to destroy him. Quevedo accepts the challenge, though Spain's major intellects and grandees—among them Ruis de Alarcón, Pacheco de Narváez, and, above all, Góngora— have signed an inflammatory petition against Lope. The third scene shows Quevedo defending a prostitute, Moscatela, against the ruffian pimp who is "her man"; he invites the woman into his home, but unwittingly insults her when he offers her a doubloon as an act of kindness. She, thinking it a charity, refuses it and goes out into the night to find her man. Montalbán, the bookseller of scene 2, returns in the fourth scene to advise Quevedo that his defense of Lope has been all too successful. All the bile that Lope's enemies had turned on him is now directed at Quevedo. Quevedo is not surprised; he is aware of the courtly intrigue that would exclude his genius—Fray Antolín, the censor, has refused to allow publication of his *Sueños* (Dreams). When Montalbán leaves, Quevedo falls into a feverish sleep and dreams. These dreams—scenes from his *Sueños*—are briefly represented on the stage.

The second period takes place twenty years later. In scene 5, Quevedo receives a visit from a former lover, the beautiful Monna Laura from Italy. She, fearing for Quevedo since the wheel of fortune has already crushed the Duke of Osuna, whom Quevedo had served and whose confidence he had enjoyed, attempts to lure him back to Italy. The court is presently in turmoil over a note that King Philip found at dinner wrapped in the napkin next to his plate—a satirical verse denouncing the excesses of the court favorite, the Count-Duke of Olivares. And the latter, she is sure, will stop at nothing to find the author of the satire. Knowing that Quevedo is that author, Laura begs him to flee. Her fears are not without foundation, for in the moment of her pleading, officers from the royal guard enter and arrest Quevedo by order of the Count-Duke of Olivares.

In the sixth scene, Quevedo is taken to the royal palace, where he meets Monna Laura once more. It is December, and Quevedo, chronically cold, is susceptible when she again offers him asylum in Italy, finally agreeing to deny authorship of the verse and go with her. As she leaves to await him in her carriage, the Count-Duke enters, asking Quevedo to analyze the poem the King found at his dinner table. This Quevedo does, revealing also that he is the author. The Count-Duke attempts to buy Quevedo, offering him an appointment as ambassador at Genoa if he will join the Count-Duke's camp. The alternative: to suffer the cold and loneliness of a cell in the dungeons of the convent of San Marcos in Leon. Notwithstanding his promise to Monna Laura and his mortal fear and hatred of the cold, Quevedo's honor chooses the convent. Scene 7 finds Quevedo returning from prison four years later to the house of a friend, where he meets Sanchica, the servants' niece, who acts as his page. She is an unspoiled, sensitive girl whom Quevedo regards as the one pure soul he has known. Quevedo dies in scene 8 with Sanchica, whom he has come to love with the platonic purity his age and infirmity require, weeping for him.

Historical Background

It seems normal that anyone studying this play will deal with the liberties Casona has taken with history, justifiable license, of course, as the author is less interested in matters of fact than matters of spiritual reality. Here and elsewhere, Casona embroiders upon historical facts as it suits his dramatic purpose. "Beauty is another form of truth," one of his characters has said. Such an artifice, for example, as Quevedo's chronic preoccupation with the cold prepares the audience to view his sentence to the dungeons of San Marcos as the cruelest form of punishment the conceited Count-Duke might devise. History records the Count-Duke's cruelty; Casona compresses it into this one calculated act of inhumanity.

Further synthesis of Casona's procedure will emerge from a discussion of his handling of the confrontation between Quevedo and Pacheco de Narváez. Luis Astrana Marín, scholar and accomplished biographer, explains that the incident, in point of historical fact, occurred during a session of the academy organized toward the end of the year 1608 by Don Pedro Manso, president of Castille. To this session, held in the house of the Count of Miranda, had come many illustrious gentlemen, among them the Duke of Osuna, Francisco de Quevedo, and Pacheco de Narváez. The latter had written a book with a long and pretentious title that dealt with the "science" of fencing. Without mentioning the title of Pacheco's book, Quevedo had debunked the general theory in his *El sueño del juicio final* (The dream of the final judgment), so it should scarcely be surprising that a certain enmity had already begun between the two men. Marín points out the details of the confrontation between them, as Pacheco, in the midst of the august academy group, is obliged to defend his thesis:

In that session of the academy of the President of Castille . . . it was inevitable that they should broach the topic of "true dexterity

founded on science," which that book [by Pacheco] . . . advanced. Especially one of the *conclusions,* which had to do with a type of attack that, according to Pacheco de Narváez, could not be parried and for which there was no defense. Quevedo contradicted him. The fencing master answered in defense of his thesis. The discussion became heated. Don Francisco waived argument in favor of practice. And for proof (writes Tarsia) he invited the master to cross swords with him; the master, although he declined alleging that the academy had come together to fight with reason and not with swords, was obliged by the other gentlemen to unsheath his sword; and at the first encounter Don Francisco struck him on the head, knocking off his hat. Narváez withdrew, quite angered by the event, and Don Francisco, adding spice to the party said: "Don Luis Pacheco proved his thesis very well; if there had been a defense for this attack, I would not have struck him."
They were from that time on mortal enemies.[11]

For many reasons, Casona has these circumstances develop not in the somber formality of the academy but amidst a certain ribaldry, natural to a tavern. He can synthesize the past in the present much more effectively by having Quevedo return from a long absence. Naturally, his friends would be interested in his activities and would question him at length—hardly the most likely topic in a sedate academy, but just the sort of expository data the audience needs. The formalized nature of the academy is suggested, however slightly, by the organization of the Brotherhood of Laughter. The joviality of the group, more important in this case than the formality, can develop far more broadly in the environment of the tavern. Moreover, the aggregate of personalities—Doña-Doña, the old barmaid and panderess, the stranger who quietly seeks her services, the soldiers, the members of the Brotherhood, the innkeeper, Pacheco, all with the catalytic presence of Quevedo—distills for the audience the spirit of the time.

In Casona's presentation of the story, unity, as we normally define it, is absent. There is no unity beyond that supplied by the compelling personality of Quevedo. In scene 3, for example, the intriguing prostitute Moscatela seems about to fill a void for Quevedo, remedying his solitude with her femininity. But she moves out of his house and his life, symbolic of the many relationships that left Quevedo unrequited. And she is typical, as few characters appear in more than one scene. But there is method in the playwright's madness. The disjointed action, the broad spectrum of characters—in short, the very lack of unity in the play is itself articulate. It bespeaks the unfettered but lonely nature of Don Francisco, and sets him apart—pits him against the society he hated in the Spain he loved. This picaresque disunion becomes, then, another testimonial to Casona's impeccable dramatic instinct.

Aesthetic Aspects

Victor Hugo's comments on the purpose of drama from the famous "Préface de Cromwell" (Preface to Cromwell) provide at once a convenient summary of Casona's purpose and our statement of how well he accomplished it:

> The stage is an optical point. Everything that exists in the world—in history, in life, in man—should be and can be reflected therein, but under the magic wand of art. Art turns the leaves of the ages, of nature, studies chronicles, strives to reproduce actual facts (especially in respect to manners and peculiarities, which are much less exposed to doubt and contradiction than are concrete facts), restores what the chroniclers have lopped off, harmonises what they have collected, divines and supplies their omissions, fills their gaps with imaginary scenes which have the colour of the time, groups what they have left scattered about, sets in motion anew the threads of Providence which work the human marionettes, clothes the whole with a form at once poetical and natural, and imparts to it that vitality of truth and brilliancy which gives birth to illusion, that prestige of reality which arouses the enthusiasm of the spectator, and of the poet first of all, for the poet is sincere. Thus the aim of art is almost divine: to bring to life again if it is writing history, to create if it is writing poetry.[12]

The fact that it is Victor Hugo, the great romantic, who wrote these thoughts suggests another aspect of *El caballero de las espuelas de oro* that seems most arresting: its similarity in concept and execution to the work that perhaps most admirably incorporates all the tenets of Hugo's romanticism, Edmond Rostand's *Cyrano de Bergerac,* the most resoundingly successful play of the last half of nineteenth-century France. Casona himself justifies a view of his works in terms of "romanticism." In his essay

Historical Plays

"Galdós y el romanticismo" ("Galdós and romanticism") he says:

> In its broadest sense, romanticism is not the exclusive emphasis of a definite period, but a rebellious "constant" in the history of the spirit, characterized by the violent opposition of man against society, free will face to face with dogma, sentiment against reason, personality against hierarchy. It is, in fine, the left wing of culture, present to some degree in all periods. Therefore, one can speak legitimately of the essential romanticism of Lope de Vega or Shakespeare, and consider Don Quijote as the most complete model of the romantic gentleman.[13]

The first similarity that strikes us in this comparison between Cyrano and Quevedo is, naturally, the obvious fact that both protagonists are seventeenth-century nonconformists. Quevedo exemplifies the same romantic blend of the grotesque and the sublime as Rostand's Cyrano. The latter, with a nose so long that it "marches on before [him] by a quarter of an hour," has a soul so sensitive, an intellect so bright, and a wit so keen that he overshadows all the men of his generation. Likewise, Quevedo, crippled and shortsighted, has overcome men in mortal confrontations, and humiliates with his sword Spain's most eminent swordsman. Moreover, he is capable of moving Monna Laura to affirm fervently that he has composed "the most beautiful love sonnet that has ever been written in your language or in mine." Cyrano's words move his beloved Roxane to tears, though she does not know the words are his.

The two protagonists are on a par in their sensitivity or vulnerability concerning their physical imperfections. When Pacheco, after Quevedo's wit has laid him bare, calls Quevedo a "poor cripple," the latter answers, "You have uttered a word that only I have a right to utter." Cyrano, in answering the Vicomte de Valvert, who has made a point of insulting him by telling him obtusely, "Your nose is . . . rather large," first ridicules Valvert for having thrown away a chance to insult him beautifully, then points out all the things he might have said, and finally reminds him, "I say these things / Lightly enough myself, about myself, / But I allow none else to utter them." In both Casona's and Rostand's plays, a duel follows.

Both protagonists place a premium on the ability to improvise, and both are careful to demonstrate their own prodigious accomplishments in this regard. Quevedo, on the spur of the moment, composes "three guffaws" to Góngora, a masterpiece of parody on *culteranismo* (roughly akin to euphuism in England, *préciosité* in France); Cyrano, among other things, composes a ballad while dueling with Valvert. Neither of the heroes blanches at facing overwhelming odds, either with the pen or the sword. Both set out to defend a friend who is threatened by certain highly placed individuals. The drunken Ligniere in *Cyrano de Bergerac* is threatened by the Count de Guiche and a band of hired assassins, Lope in *El caballero de las espuelas de oro* by a host of grandees and intellectuals. Quevedo's golden spurs, which he will wear at his death to "walk with dignity in the Kingdom of God," parallel Cyrano's white plume, which (he says) is the one crown he can bear away to heaven, where his salute shall "sweep all the stars from the blue threshold." Finally, each dies with the woman he loves, unattainable still, weeping for him. And death has cheated both of them, or so they suppose, of the fulfillment of which they dreamed.

Little wonder that Quevedo, "characterized by the violent opposition of men against society, free will face to face with dogma, sentiment against reason, personality against hierarchy," should appeal to Casona, suspicious as the playwright was of our dehumanized society, and committed as he was to the sacredness of individual dignity and the brotherhood of man. His admiration led him, years before the actual composition of the play, to the idea of dramatizing the life of Quevedo, an idea that found its expression during the author's maturity and became the "mellow fruit of [his] wisdom."[14] The first performance of the play in Barcelona, July 14, 1964, was the occasion for Casona's auto-critique, wherein his own admiration for Quevedo's fierce individuality and sensitivity shows through:

Don Francisco de Quevedo, so rich in inventions, is also the inventor of "the Spanish fury." His insolence as a swordsman-poet, his aggressiveness against any falsification in life or in literature, the dazzling wit of his laughter, and his sudden outbursts of satire and mysticism are his real "golden spurs," the spurs which he used to prick the flanks of his times (the actual pair of golden spurs he kept were stolen and misused just after his death). Quevedo, a great solitary amid the

Baroque clamor of the Golden Age—the "gold" of the times being more a sign of autumnal decline than a symbol of glory—is without a doubt, the most dramatic figure in our literary history. His life shows us a cross-section of Spain under the last of the Hapsburgs, and exposes the entrails of the nation—still trembling with fervor but half decayed by corruption. Quevedo (a great squanderer of the language) feels, in his unique way, that the glorious nation his generation inherited from their ancestors is like a living history which is slowly being deprived of a territory in which to take place. Thus, he comes to the rescue to try to avoid total disaster, fighting decadence and corruption. To this end he devotes all of his efforts, utilizing whatever means he is capable of: satire and warning, accusation and sarcasm, violent insult and desperate plea. No one else has ever so fully expressed a nationality. There is not a single great Spanish passion which is not present in Quevedo in its full force: pride, honor, rebelliousness, thirst for adventure, and mysticism. And he embodies all of these passions in such a way that he is still alive in them, and by them he continues to dominate the scene and keeps on teaching us. Quevedo is not in the museum; he is out in the open, on the streets, in the people. This is why I have attempted to create a "dramatic portrait," for which we had such a need.[15]

Clearly Quevedo is more than a man for Casona; he is a symbol embodying something of his own love and grief for Spain.

Chapter Six
Summation

Casona came into mortality in the wake of *fin-de-siècle* skepticism, with its overload of pessimism spawned by the nineteenth century's marriage to concepts of biological evolution. He joins the many who feel that our mechanized society is dehumanizing and chants with the chorus that decries the predominance of science over spirituality. He feels that man, lacking empathic imagination, is too prone to deal with vital human problems on the basis of pure abstractions and too often unable to sympathize actively with *el dolor ajeno* ("someone else's problems"). Thus, man's lack of imagination constitutes a sin against Love, which for Casona is one of the "three great words"; the other two are God and Death.[1] Many have noted the prevalence of fantasy in Casona's works, the interplay of fantasy and reality, fantasy and illusion. Certain "other-worldly" characters, notably the Devil and Death, are familiar to those who know Casona's theater. These characters simultaneously possess supernatural qualities and human tendencies and emotions. Casona's Devil is a *pobre diablo,* a pathetic figure with modest supernatural powers, which are never as conspicuous as his humanity. For the most part, Casona's views parallel those of his contemporary Giovanni Papini, who asserts that there would be no saintliness without the Devil; there must be opposition in order to achieve glory, for without battle, there can be no victory.[2]

Death too is imbued with humanity. Casona does not choose to follow the macabre tradition; he personifies Death as a woman distressed at the apparently tragic nature of her mission. Like his baroque predecessor Gracián, Casona points out that the tragedy conventionally associated with her is relative, for, as the Peregrina herself suggests, she is a friend to the poor and to men of clear conscience, for whom death may represent a fulfillment. It is not possible to determine to what extent Casona accepts as valid such phenomena as ESP, but the importance accorded to it in many of his plays again suggests a plea for a more imaginative approach to life, since its existence refutes positivistic determinism and modern science based on mathematical symbolism, wherein life and nature are apprehended by means of their parts and described in numerical formulas.

The principal touchstone of fantasy in three of Casona's plays is the establishment of rare institutions. In *La sirena varada* an attempt is made to form a republic for persons devoid of common sense. Dr. Ariel, an individual never seen, founds what is ostensibly a suicide home in *Prohibido suicidarse en primavera,* and in *Los árboles mueren de pie* he organizes an institution dedicated to providing a moment of happiness for unfortunate souls. The proposed republic in *La sirena varada* is organized out of rebellion against prevailing materialism. The other two institutions are founded to provide a cure for the victims of such a society. All three are established for a noble purpose, but in every case they succumb to the very influences they are trying to avoid or remedy, for, as time goes on, there is a tendency on the part of the directing authority to accord greater importance to their respective organizations than to the individual they were meant to serve. Individual problems do not readily accommodate themselves to man-made rules and regulations.

Many of Casona's characters subjectively withdraw from the society that sets human values aside. While Casona would agree with their censure of that society, he does not agree with their attempt to escape life's responsibilities. For him, life is a duty. He enjoins humanity to view it with imagination and awaken its latent sympathy for *el dolor ajeno,* the problems of others, thus to mitigate the tendency toward dehumanization, but he continues to sustain the innate worth of man and his inherent dignity. Charles Leighton points out that for Casona illusion is justifiable only insofar as it serves humanity, or leads to some truth, and we must add emphatically that this includes artistic truth. Casona would agree with Socrates that the good, the true, and the beautiful are synonymous.

Casona masters all the common devices for creating humor; conflict, contrast, incongruity, repetition, and inversion, to mention just a few, are exemplary. He is also fond of equivocal situations, which involve dramatic irony, implication, and play on words. Often these devices serve a greater mistress, a gentle satire, which is ethically or aesthetically corrective. Wherever human frailty is criticized humorously, it may be said that satire is present to some degree, and Casona's humor is most frequently calculated to expose some human excess or deficiency, thus further revealing his preoccupation with the balance of human values in society. Perhaps it can be argued that all humor is essentially based upon a sense of balance. Henri Bergson's theories substantiate such a postulation.

Ever concerned with the spiritual side of man, Casona has a strong faith in the ultimate goodness of the "people," hence the lessons of legend, folklore, and history have captivated his fancy. His most recent works, concluded just prior to his death, were a historical play, the story of Francisco de Quevedo (*El caballero de las espuelas de oro*), and a version of the famous Renaissance dramatic novel, the *Celestina*. A great majority of his works are based upon traditional materials—materials that "emanate from the people" and "have the power to return to them." As seen in his dramatization of the folk tale of *La molinera de Arcos,* in the blend of history and legend in his *Corona de amor y muerte,* and his treatment of the perennial questions of death and evil, specifically in his plays *Otra vez el Diablo, La barca sin pescador,* and *La dama del alba,* Casona treats universal and eternal themes. He is clearly allegorical in his play *Siete gritos en el mar.*

Recent critics, waving the banners of social theater and riding the bandwagon of the *engagés,* have not spoken kindly of Casona's works. Following the overwhelming reception of his plays in Spain during the 1960s, critics began to accuse Casona of holding naive and antiquated ideals; or, failing to grasp that such ideals are even tenable in a modern context, they accuse him of insincerity. Unfortunately, as the wheel of fortune turns for these critics, it crushes the champion of the "old-fashioned" values. Casona's theater no longer commands the almost unanimous critical approval it once did. It appears that his detractors, at least for the moment, have outshouted his defenders. Perhaps, in a distant utopia, when the clamor of the existential pharisees subsides, the world will return to the comfortable sanity of old-fashioned ideals, and Casona, by dint of a dramatic technique that needs no defense, may "rise again."

Notes and References

Chapter One

1. See J. Rodríguez Richart, *Vida y teatro de Alejandro Casona* (Oviedo, 1963), p. 11. For this chapter, I rely heavily upon Rodríguez Richart. I have also drawn extensively upon Charles H. Leighton, "Alejandro Casona and the New Theater in Spain," Ph.D. diss., Harvard University, 1961; William H. Shoemaker's "Introduction" to *Nuestra Natacha* (see note 3); and Constantino Suárez's *Escritores y artistas asturianos* (see note 5).
2. *Casona:* "large house," or "mansion."
3. See William H. Shoemaker's "Introduction" to his school edition of Casona's *Nuestra Natacha* (New York, 1947), p. xiii.
4. César Tiempo, "Con Alejandro Casona," *El Radical* (Buenos Aires), June 23, 1945.
5. Angel Lázaro, "Los que triunfan en plena juventud: Alejandro Casona," *Crónica* (Madrid), May 6, 1934. Cited by Constantino Suárez, *Escritores y artistas asturianos, índice bio-bibliográfico* (Oviedo: Instituto de Estudios Asturianos), P-R, 6:495.
6. Rodríguez Richart, *Vida,* p. 13.
7. Ibid., p. 14.
8. *Obras completas* (Madrid, 1967), p. xii.
9. Juan José Plans, *Alejandro Casona* (Oviedo, 1965), p. 60.
10. Rodríguez Richart, *Vida,* p. 15.
11. Angel Lázaro, cited by Suárez, *Escritores,* p. 469.
12. Plans, *Casona,* p. 70.
13. *La barca sin pescador,* ed. José A. Balseiro and J. Riis Owre (New York, 1955), pp. xii–xiii.
14. Plans, *Casona,* p. 71.
15. *La barca sin pescador,* ed. Balseiro and Owre, pp. xiii, xvi.
16. The date for the completion of this play was established by Casona himself in a letter to Charles H. Leighton dated July 13, 1959. See Leighton, "Alejandro Casona," p. 12.
17. Greater detail can be found in José Balseiro, "Alejandro Casona," *El Mundo* (San Juan de Puerto Rico), June 29, 1941.
18. Lolo de la Torriente, "Alejandro Casona en México," *Excelsior* (México, D.F.), June 2, 1937, p. 8.
19. José María Souviron, *La nueva poesía española* (Santiago de Chile: Editorial Nascimento, 1932), p. 46.

20. Rodríguez Richart, *Vida*, p. 19.
21. Suárez, *Escritores*, p. 493.
22. Plans, *Casona*, pp. 73–74.
23. Inspección Provincial de Madrid: "Provincial Inspection Bureau."
24. [*Memoria del*] *Patronato de Misiones Pedagógicas. Septiembre de 1931/diciembre de 1933* (Madrid: Patronato de Misiones Pedagógicas, 1934), part 2, chapter 3, "Misiones realizadas," pp. 16–29, and chapter 4, "Dicen los misioneros," pp. 29–59. Cited by Leighton, "Alejandro Casona," p. 17.
25. *Teatro del Pueblo:* "Theater of the People."
26. Shoemaker, "Introduction," pp. xvii–xviii.
27. See Enrique Díez Canedo, "The Contemporary Spanish Theater," in *The Theater of a Changing Europe,* ed. Thomas H. Dickenson (New York: Henry Holt, 1937), pp. 315–16.
28. *Retablo jovial* (Buenos Aires, 1949), pp. 10–11.
29. Díez-Canedo, "Contemporary," lists thirteen titles; Shoemaker, "Introduction," p. xviii, lists only twelve.
30. See Suárez, *Escritores,* p. 499. Leighton, "Alejandro Casona," p. 20, in an effort to get further information on those speeches, wrote to Casona and received the following reply: "As for my lectures, it is useless (and it would be totally boring) to specify them. Aside from those you allude to [those cited by Suárez] I probably gave a hundred lectures in theaters, universities, athenaeums and cultural institutions of Spain, México, Cuba, Puerto Rico, Colombia, Venezuela, Chile, Argentina and Uruguay on the following themes: 'Teatro social' ('Social Theater'), 'Poesía nueva' ('New Poetry'), 'Teatro clásico español' ('Classic Spanish Theater'), 'Lope de Vega: vida y amores' ('Lope de Vega: His Life and Loves'), 'El diablo en la literatura' ('The Devil in Literature'), 'El amor en la poesía' (Love in Poetry'), 'El amor en la historia' ('Love in History'), 'Geografía del amor' ('The Geography of Love'), 'Teatro para el pueblo' ('Theater for the People'), etc. Sometimes, when I had access to a theater and an adequate theme, they were lecture-demonstrations, enlivened with presentations of scenes by Lope, Tirso, Calderón, Cervantes." Letter dated July 13, 1959. Most of the lectures Casona refers to would have been delivered much later than the time during which he was involved with the *Patronato.*
31. Suárez, *Escritores,* p. 500. In the same letter of July 13, 1959, Casona informed Mr. Leighton, "Surely Suárez (who was an excellent personal friend and a very meticulous man) is right in noting my contributions to those magazines. . . ." As Leighton points out, Suárez was not meticulous enough, for he provided no specific references to the periodicals in question. "Casona himself," says Leighton, "admit-

ted that he could be of little help in such matters. Later in the same letter he said, characteristically enough: 'And please, don't ask me for any more specific data. I have a horror of filing cabinets—which is no virtue, but it is respectable'" Leighton, "Alejandro Casona," p. 20.

32. Pedro Salinas, writing in *Indice* (Madrid) in 1934, gives us this number. Casona himself told both Marino Gómez Santos and José Plans that there were six hundred entries.

33. Angel Lázaro, cited by Suárez, *Escritores,* p. 501.

34. Antonio Espina, review of *Otra vez el Diablo, El Sol* (Madrid), April 27, 1935. Cited in *Indice Literario* (Madrid) 4, no. 6 (June 1935):131.

35. For example, see Enrique Díez-Canedo's review of *Otra vez el Diablo, La Voz* (Madrid), April 27, 1935. Cited in *Indice Literario* (Madrid) 4, no. 6 (June 1935):131.

36. Shoemaker, "Introduction," pp. xxv–xxvi.

37. Ibid., p. xxiv.

38. *La barca sin pescador,* ed. Balseiro and Owre, p. xx (based on a letter from Casona to Balseiro dated January 30, 1938).

39. *Obras completas* (Madrid, 1967), 1:61–62.

40. "*Romance de Dan y Elsa.* Estrenó anoche la compañía M. Ortiz," *La Prensa* (Buenos Aires), September 16, 1939, p. 14.

41. *La barca sin pescador,* ed. Balseiro and Owre, pp. xxi–xxii.

42. See note 30 above. See also Shoemaker, "Introduction," p. xxvi.

43. "*Las tres perfectas casadas* no es una obra original," *ABC* (Madrid), October 4, 1950. Cited by Rodríguez Richart, p. 148.

44. "Una carta del señor Casona," *ABC, Edicion semanal aérea* (Madrid), November 9, 1950, p. 25.

45. See, for example, the critique in *La Prensa* (Buenos Aires) that followed the play's premiere, "Lola Membrives estrenó *Las tres perfectas casadas,"* April 19, 1941, p. 16.

46. José Caso González, "Fantasía y realidad en el teatro de Alejandro Casona," *Archivum, Revista de la Facultad de Filosofía y Letras* (Oviedo) (nueva serie) 5 (1955):311.

47. From a letter to William H. Shoemaker dated March 24, 1946. Shoemaker, "Introduction," p. xxviii.

48. *Obras completas,* 1:82.

49. "Muy grata comedia en el Teatro Ateneo," *La Prensa* (Buenos Aires), April 2, 1949, p. 7.

50. Review of *Los árboles mueren de pie, Württembergische Abendseitung* (Stuttgart), November 14, 1950. Cited by Juan Rodríguez Castellano in his school edition of *Los árboles mueren de pie* (New York, 1953), p. xxii.

51. Cited in *La barca sin pescador,* ed. Balseiro and Owre, p. xxiii.

52. Just as the primitive religious theater (*autos* or *misterios*) dramatized biblical passages and other liturgical themes, the popular theater developed along the lines of customs or coarse humor. These farcical representations were called *juegos de escarnio. Paso* was the name given by Lope de Rueda (d. 1565) to a type of brief farce. The *pasos* are the immediate ancestors of the *entremés,* which is a short farce, designed to be presented between the first and second acts of a full-length *comedia* or drama.

53. This work is included in *Obras completas,* 2:963-1063.

54. Cited in *La barca sin pescador,* ed. Balseiro and Owre, p. xxiii.

55. Letter to Rodríguez Castellano dated April 15, 1952. Cited in *Los árboles mueren de pie,* ed. Rodríguez Castellano, p. xxi.

56. The name *auto* is one of the earliest to appear in Spanish literature. It originally defined a diversity of theatrical presentations, both religious and profane. In the Middle Ages, the *autos* became synonymous with the "mystery" and "morality" plays. In the second half of the sixteenth century they acquired the name *auto sacramental* and dealt exclusively with religious themes. The *auto* is inevitably allegorical.

57. *Obras completas,* 1:90-91.

58. Ibid., pp. 98-99. Cf. *La barca sin pescador,* ed. Balseiro and Owre, pp. xxiii-xxiv.

59. *Obras completas,* 2:674.

60. "Luisa Vehil se presentará hoy en el T. Liceo," *La Nación* (Buenos Aires), April 12, 1957, p. 8.

61. "Se estrenó en el Liceo una obra de Casona," *La Nación* (Buenos Aires), April 13, 1957, p. 7.

62. *Obras completas,* 2:70-71.

63. In a letter to the author dated March 17, 1959, Casona mentions that he had recently written the play (". . . que escribí hace poco"), and that, since it had at that time not been performed, it was not to be included in the current edition of his complete works. Now, of course, it appears in vol. 2 of the 1967 edition of *Obras completas,* pp. 347-423.

64. Leighton, "Alejandro Casona," p. 53.

65. José A. Balseiro and Eliana Suárez-Rivero affirm that "no other Spanish playwright ever had such a number of his plays presented simultaneously in so many theaters, in his own country and around the world." See their "Introduction" to the school edition of *El caballero de las espuelas de oro* (New York, 1968), pp. x, xxxii.

Notes and References 135

66. "Estreno de *El caballero de las espuelas de oro,* de Casona, en el Bellas Artes," *ABC* (Madrid), October 2, 1964, p. 79.
67. See Federico Carlos Sainz de Robles's "Prólogo," in the 1967 edition of *Obras completas,* p. xxx.
68. Balseiro and Suárez-Rivero, "Introduction," p. xxxiv.

Chapter Two

1. From a letter I received dated March 17, 1959.
2. Alejandro Casona, *Obras completas* (Mexico: Aguilar, 1954), 1:1167.
3. Lee Leighton, "Alejandro Casona and the New Theater," pp. 213, 250–52.
4. See Sainz de Robles's "Introduction" to *Alejandro Casona, Obras completas,* especially pp. 91–92.
5. Pedro A. de Alarcón, *El capitán Veneno y El sombrero de tres picos* (Buenos Aires: Austral, 1957), p. 71. The translation is mine.
6. Alejandro Casona, *Obras completas,* p. 694.
7. The translation of "Fiscala" is "the district attorney's wife"—obviously too cumbersome to use in the text. Comandanta translates as "the commander's wife"; Corregidora, "the Corregidor's wife." I have retained the more docile Spanish forms.
8. The translation is Martin Armstrong's. His version of Alarcón's tale appears in *Great Spanish Stories,* ed. Angel Flores (New York: Modern Library, 1956), pp. 20–112. I use his translation throughout, except in the rare instances where, for varying reasons (always indicated with a note reference), I use my own.
9. Henri Bergson, *Laughter, An Essay on the Meaning of the Comic* (London: Macmillan, 1911), p. 94.
10. Alejandro Casona, *Obras completas,* p. 80.
11. This portion does not appear in the version included in *Great Spanish Stories.* The translation is mine.
12. "Dulce enemiga," *Indice Literario, Suplemento de El Universal* (Caracas), March 27, 1956, p. 4.
13. "Yo pecador," *Indice Literario,* June 2, 1959, p. 4.
14. Charles H. Leighton has collected most of these dates in his article "Alejandro Casona and the Devil," *Hispania* 48 (1965):29. See also in the same issue of *Hispania* my article "Calderón and Casona," note 2, p. 42.
15. Wilfred L. Guerin et al., *A Handbook of Critical Approaches to Literature* (New York: Harper & Row, 1966), p. 118.
16. Giovanni Papini, *The Devil* (London: Eyre & Spottiswoode, 1955), p. 148.

17. *Indice Literario,* August 20, 1959, p. 3. See also Leighton, "Alejandro Casona and the New Theater," p. 301. Leighton points out that the devil traditionally occupies himself in denying everything the Catholic fathers have alleged.
18. *Alejandro Casona, Obras completas,* p. 21.
19. "Don Juan y el Diablo," *Cuadernos del Congreso por la Libertad de la Cultura* (Paris), January-February 1956, pp. 69–70.
20. Bergson, *Laughter,* pp. 125–26.
21. Ibid., pp. 177–78.
22. Ibid., p. 96.
23. Ibid., p. 179.
24. William Rose Benet, ed., *The Reader's Encyclopedia* (New York: Thomas Y. Crowell, 1948), p. 544.
25. Joseph T. Shipley, ed., *Dictionary of World Literature* (New York: Philosophical Library), 1953, p. 331.
26. Walter Blair, John Gerber, and Eugene Garber, *Better Reading Two: Literature* (Chicago: Scott, Foresman, 1966), p. 78.
27. See Casona's essay "El niño y su mentira," *Indice Literario,* May 29, 1956, p. 1.
28. J. Rodríguez-Richart, "Imaginación y realismo en el teatro: *La barca sin pescador* de Casona," *Boletín de la biblioteca Menéndez Pelayo* 39 (1963):236–37.
29. Ibid., pp. 235–36.
30. Charles H. Leighton, "Casona, McLuhan and Utopia," an unpublished paper Dr. Leighton was kind enough to show me.
31. Mircea Eliade, *The Sacred and the Profane,* trans. Willard R. Trask (New York: Harper & Row, 1961), p. 203.
32. Arnold Reichenberger, "The Uniqueness of the Comedia," *Hispanic Review* 27 (1959):306.
33. Robert G. Hunter, *Shakespeare and the Comedy of Forgiveness* (New York: Columbia University Press, 1965), p. 48.
34. Ibid., p. 13.
35. Ibid., p. 12.
36. Ibid., p. 39.
37. Reichenberger, "Uniqueness," p. 307.
38. Hunter, *Shakespeare,* p. 7.
39. Ibid.
40. L. W. Keats, "Mysterious Miraculous Mandarin," *Revue de Littérature Comparée* 40 (1966):517–19.
41. Francisco Ruiz Ramón, *Historia del teatro español* (Madrid, 1971), 2:257–58.
42. Hunter, *Shakespeare,* p. 84.
43. Keats, "Mysterious," p. 520.
44. Hunter, *Shakespeare,* p. 39.

Notes and References

45. Ibid., p. 37.
46. Ibid.
47. Ibid., pp. 243–44.
48. Northrop Frye, *Anatomy of Criticism* (New York: Atheneum, 1969), p. 162.
49. Hunter, *Shakespeare,* p. 3.
50. Ibid., p. 112.
51. Ibid., pp. 58–59.
52. Ibid., p. 48.
53. Frye, *Anatomy,* p. 179.
54. Hunter, *Shakespeare,* p. 70.
55. See Harold Bayley, *The Lost Language of Symbolism* (London: Barnes & Noble, 1912), chapter 10. The following from the Arcipreste de Hita's *Libro de buen amor* offers a case in point (italics mine):

> ¡Virgen santa!
> . . . .
> ¡*Estrella de la mar!*
> ¡*Puerto de fulgura!*
> ¡De dolor é pasar
> E de tristura
> Vénme librar
> E confortar,
> Señora, del altura!

56. See Charles H. Leighton, "Casona and Lorca: A Brief Comparison," *Modern Drama* 7 (1964):31.
57. Juan R. Castellano, "Casona y Asturias," *Hispania* 25 (1952):392.
58. Joaquín de Entrambasaguas, "El teatro de Alejandro Casona," *Clavileño* (Madrid) 4 (July-August 1950):34–36.
59. Pablo de A. Cobos, "Algunas constantes en el teatro de A. Casona," *Insula* 155 (October 1959):4.
60. In *Prohibido suicidarse en primavera,* Casona has Chole tell Dr. Roda, director of the suicide home, "La muerte es más hábil que ustedes," and in *Corona de amor y muerte,* Prince Pedro asks Inés, who visits him after her death, if she is far away. She answers, "¡Aquí mismo, pero tan separados! Tú, en el lado de todas las preguntas; yo, en el de la única contestación."

Chapter Three

1. Frank Sedwick says, appropriately, ". . . the linking of Pirandello's name with another author has become a twentieth-century liter-

ary occupation, even though 'influence' is in the terrain of occasional mirages." "Unamuno and Pirandello Revisited," *Italica* 32 (1956):40.

2. W. Somerset Maugham has said that solipsism is ". . . a theory that can hardly fail to allure the writer of fiction. The claims it makes are his common practice. It has a completeness and an elegance that make it infinitely attractive." *The Summing Up* (London: William Heinemann, 1938), p. 265.

3. Charles H. Leighton, "Alejandro Casona's 'Pirandellism,' " *Symposium* 17 (1963):212.

4. See *Indice Literario, Suplemento de El Universal* (Caracas), February 5, 1957, p. 1.

5. J. L. C., "Charla con Alejandro Casona," *Insula,* no. 191 (October 1962):5.

6. See *Revista de esudios hispánicos* 1 (November 1967):189-90.

7. For example, A. W. Woolsey says, "We can only reach the conclusion that the author feels that there is no escape other than to face reality. An illusory or imaginary way of life must fade away in the pitiless light of reality." "Illusion versus Reality in Some of the Plays of Alejandro Casona," *Modern Language Journal* 38 (1954):84.

8. For greater detail on this subject see Charles H. Leighton, "Alejandro Casona and the Revolt against Reason," *Modern Language Journal* 46 (1962):56-61.

9. Eric Bentley, *In Search of Theater* (New York: Knopf, 1953), p. 309.

10. Casona's play on the words *salto mortal* ("somersault") completely defies exact translation.

11. Bergson, *Laughter,* p. 69.

12. Harry Allen Overstreet, *About Ourselves* (New York: W. W. Norton, 1927), p. 260.

13. Charles Leighton, "Alejandro Casona y las ideas," *Insula,* no. 206 (January 1964):15.

14. See my article "Alejandro Casona and Henri Bergson," in *Spanish Thought and Letters in the Twentieth Century,* ed. Germán Bleiberg and E. Inman Fox (Nashville, 1966), pp. 345-59.

15. Ricardo Doménech, among others with whom we have dealt in earlier pages, denies that Casona has a place in the mainstream of current thought. See "Para un arreglo de cuentas con el teatro de Alejandro Casona," *Insula,* no. 209 (April 1964):15.

Chapter Four

1. *Indice Literario, Suplemento de El Universal* (Caracas), May 6, 1958, p. 4.

2. From a letter to Charles H. Leighton, dated May 21, 1960,

quoted in Mr. Leighton's article "Alejandro Casona and the Significance of Dreams," *Hispania* 45 (December 1962):700.

Chapter Five

1. For many of the thoughts in this section—and even for many of the words—I owe a great debt to a former graduate student, Karen Lynn, whose master's thesis consisted of an English translation of *Corona de amor y muerte* and a critical introduction. I am grateful to her for her kind permission to use her material.
2. For greater detail, see the student edition of *Corona de amor y muerte* prepared by José A. Balseiro and J. Riis Owre, especially their "Introduction" (New York: Oxford University Press, 1960), pp. ix–xxvii.
3. Fernán López, *Crónica de El-Rei D. Pedro I.* Quoted in H. V. Livermore, *A History of Portugal* (Cambridge: Cambridge University Press, 1947), pp. 162–63.
4. Charles H. Leighton, "Alejandro Casona as Essayist: The Message Finds Its Medium," *Revista de Estudios Hispánicos* 6 (1972):106.
5. "Tres sonrisas de mujer," *Indice Literario, Suplemento de El Universal* (Caracas), November 27, 1958, p. 4.
6. Leighton, "Alejandro Casona as Essayist," pp. 106–7.
7. *El Universal*, November 29, 1955, p. 1.
8. Ibid.
9. Some years ago now, I was privileged to join in a series of delightful discussions with several friends, Professor Foster among them. It was during that period that these ideas emerged.
10. Esperanza Gurza, *La realidad caleidoscópica de Alejandro Casona* (Oviedo, 1968), pp. 124–26.
11. Luis Astrana Marín, *La vida turbulenta de Quevedo* (Madrid: Editorial "Gran Capitán," 1945), pp. 149–50.
12. Victor Hugo, "Preface to Cromwell," in *Prefaces and Prologues to Famous Books*, vol. 39 of *Harvard Classics* (New York: P. F. Collier & Son, 1910), pp. 386–87.
13. "Galdós y el romanticismo," *Revista del Colegio Libre de Estudios Superiores* (Buenos Aires) 24 (October, November, December 1943):99–111.
14. See José A. Balseiro and Eliana Suárez-Rivero's "Introduction" to the school edition of *El caballero de las espuelas de oro* (New York, 1968), p. v.
15. The quotation is cited in ibid., pp. xiii–xiv. It originally appeared on the program for the performances of *El caballero de las espuelas de oro* in the Teatro Bellas Artes in Madrid.

Chapter Six

1. The observations in this concluding chapter are not, of course, new. I made many of them in my master's thesis in 1959 and subsequently in my doctoral dissertation (Syracuse University, 1963). Charles Leighton has also touched most of them in his dissertation. See especially p. 310. My wording in these pages is occasionally influenced by Mr. Leighton's work.

2. See Leighton, "Alejandro Casona and the Devil," p. 31.

Selected Bibliography

PRIMARY SOURCES

Arturo Sánchez-Rojas has compiled the most complete bibliography of Casona's works. See "Bibliografía de Alejandro Casona." *Boletín del Instituto de Estudios Asturianos* (Oviedo), no. 76 (1972):1–25. Even this effort is not exhaustive, however.

1. Collections. These appear under the name Alejandro Rodríguez Alvarez in *The National Union Catalog* in the Library of Congress, Washington, D. C., vol. 46, (1963–67), p. 245. After the first two entries, collections arranged chronologically.

Obras completas. Edited by Federico C. Saínz de Robles. 6th ed., 2 vols. Madrid: Editorial Aguilar, 1967.

Teatro selecto. Edited by Federico C. Saínz de Robles. Madrid: Editorial Escelicer, 1966.

La sirena varada, Prohibido suicidarse en primavera, Entremés del mancebo que casó con mujer brava. Buenos Aires: Losada, 1941.

La molinera de Arcos, Sinfonía inacabada. Buenos Aires: Losada, 1956.

La sirena varada, Las tres perfectas casadas, Entremés del mancebo que casó con mujer brava. Buenos Aires: Losada, 1957.

La sirena varada, La barca sin pescador, Los árboles mueren de pie. Buenos Aires: Losada, 1957.

La dama del alba, La barca sin pescador. Buenos Aires: Losada, 1964.

El caballero de las espuelas de oro, Retablo jovial. Madrid: Espasa-Calpe, 1965.

Nuestra Natacha, Otra vez el Diablo. Buenos Aires: Losada, 1965.

Retablo jovial, El caballero de las espuelas de oro. Madrid: Espasa-Calpe, 1965.

2. Editions of individual plays

Los árboles mueren de pie. Buenos Aires: Editorial Ateneo, 1949; Buenos Aires: Losada, 1951, 2d ed. 1964; New York: Henry Holt, 1953; Madrid: Escelicer, 1964.

La barca sin pescador. Buenos Aires: Losada, 1950; New York: Oxford University Press, 1955; Paris: Librairie Théatrale, 1958; Madrid: Escelicer, 1964; Madrid: Ediciones Alcalá, 1966.

El caballero de las espeulas de oro. Published in Saínz de Robles, Federico C. *Teatro Español 1964–65.* Madrid: Aguilar, 1966, pp. 125–91; New York: Oxford University Press, 1968.
La casa de los siete balcones. Madrid: Escelicer, 1966.
Corona de amor y muerte. New York: Oxford University Press, 1960. Reprinted in Saínz de Robles, Federico C. *Teatro Español 1966–67.* Madrid: Aguilar, 1968, pp. 143–219.
El crimen de Lord Arturo. México: Editorial Aguilar, 1951.
La dama del alba. Buenos Aires: Losada, 1944; New York: Charles Scribner's Sons, 1947; Buenos Aires: Renacimiento, 1951; Paris: Librairie Théatrale, 1951; Madrid: Escelicer, 1962; Madrid: Ediciones Alcalá, 1965.
La molinera de Arcos. Buenos Aires: Losada, 1948.
Nuestra Natacha. Madrid: Poveda, 1936; Madrid: Editorial Magisterio Español, 1926; Barcelona: Teatro Selecto, 1936; Buenos Aires: Argentores, 1936; Buenos Aires: Losada, 1943; New York: Appleton Century Crofts, 1947.
Otra vez el Diablo. Madrid: Rivadeneyra, 1935; Barcelona: Editorial Teatro Selecto, 1936; México: Universidad Nacional, 1937; Buenos Aires: Losada, 1943; Madrid: Escelicer, 1965.
Prohibido suicidarse en primavera. Buenos Aires: Losada, 1943, 2d ed. 1957; Buenos Aires: Editorial Renacimiento, 1951; Buenos Aires: Argentores, 1960; Madrid: Escelicer, 1965.
Retablo jovial. Buenos Aires: Librería Ateneo, 1949; Buenos Aires: Losada, 1959.
Sinfonía Inacabada. Buenos Aires: Losada, 1949; Madrid: Escelicer, 1965.
La sirena varada. Madrid: Rivadeneyra, 1934; Buenos Aires: Losada, 1941; New York: Appleton Century Crofts, 1951; Madrid: Escelicer, 1954.
La tercera palabra. Buenos Aires: Losada, 1959; Madrid: Escelicer, 1965.
Las tres perfectas casadas. Buenos Aires: Losada, 1943. Reprinted in Saínz de Robles, Federico C. *Teatro Español 1965–66.* Madrid: Aguilar, 1967, pp. 37–97.

3. Films (arranged chronologically)
Veinte años y una noche. Buenos Aires: Estudios Filmadores Argentinos, 1940. Original.
En el viejo Buenos Aires. Buenos Aires: Estudios San Miguel, 1941. Original.
La maestrita de los obreros. Buenos Aires: Estudios Filmadores Argentinos, 1941.
Concierto de almas. Buenos Aires: Estudios Baires, 1942. Original.

Ceniza al viento. Buenos Aires: Estudios Baires, 1942. Casona wrote one of the six episodes in this film.
Cuando florezca el naranjo. Buenos Aires: Estudios San Miguel, 1943. Original.
Casa de muñecas. Adaptation of Ibsen's *A Doll's House.* Buenos Aires: Estudios San Miguel, 1943.
Nuestra Natacha. Buenos Aires: Estudios San Miguel, 1943. Two earlier versions of this work appeared, one in Spain (Estudios Cifesa, 1936) and the other in Brazil, in Portuguese (1940).
El María Celeste. Buenos Aires: Estudios Sonofilm, 1944.
Le fruit mordu. In collaboration with Jules Supervielle. Adaptation of *Martine,* by J. Jacques Bernard. Chile: Andes Film, 1945.
Margarita la tornera. Buenos Aires: Estudios San Miguel, 1946.
El abuelo. Adaptation of a work by Benito Pérez Galdós. Buenos Aires: Estudios San Miguel, 1946.

4. Poetry (arranged chronologically)

El peregrino de la barba florida. Leyenda milagrosa en poesía. Madrid: Editorial Caro Raggio, 1928.
La flauta del sapo (Poesía lírica). Valle de Arán, 1930; México: Instituto de Cultura Iberoamericana, 1937.

5. Articles and essays

Table of Abbreviations:

CCLC	*Cuadernos del Congreso por la Libertad de la Cultura* (Paris)
ET	*El Tiempo* (Bogotá)
EU	*El Universal* (Caracas)
ILEU	*Indice Literario de El Universal* (Caracas)
ILSEU	*Indice Literario, Suplemento de El Universal* (Caracas)
LDSET	*Lecturas Dominicales, Suplemento Semanal de El Tiempo* (Bogotá)

1955

"Don Juan y el Diablo." EU, 19 October, p. 4.
"La casa del amor." ILSEU, 29 November, p. 1.
"Villancico y pasión." EU, 24 December, p. 4.

1956

"De la gran Celestina al Gran Galeoto." ILSEU, 17 January, p. 4.

"Pícaros y caballeros." EU, 12 February, p. 4.
"Dulce enemiga." ILSEU, 27 March, p. 4.
"Ciudad-mujer." ILSEU, 15 May, pp. 1, 3.
"El sueño de las siete ciudades." CCLC, no. 18 (May-June):16–18.
"El niño y su mentira." ILSEU, 29 May, p. 1.
"El nuevo teatro en Italia." ILSEU, 3 July, p. 4.
"La bella durmiente de Nápoles." EU, 4 September, p. 14.
"Aforismos de pan y vino." EU, 25 September, p. 14.
"Platero y Juan Ramón." ILSEU, 13 November, p. 1.
"El balcón de Julieta." EU, 5 December, p. 4.

1957

"Cantares de navidad." EU, 5 January, p. 4.
"Dos procesos sensacionales." ILSEU, 22 January, p. 1.
"¿Brujas otra vez?" ILSEU, 5 February, p. 1.
"Un minuto de eternidad." ILSEU, 5 March, p. 1.
"Ténica del ultraje." ILSEU, 2 April, p. 4.
"Galantería." ILSEU, 14 May, p. 1.
"Mentiras de sol." EU, 4 June, p. 4.
"Las siete cursis de Granada." EU, 9 July, p. 4.
"Veneno y mujer." EU, 6 August, p. 4.
"El arte de bautizar." EU, 4 September, p. 4.
"Repertorio de pecados. EU, 15 October, p. 4.
"Pueblo y teatro." EU, 6 November, p. 4.
"Estética del fracaso." EU, 4 December, p. 4.

1958

"Famosos disparates." EU, 5 January, p. 4.
"Amigos de cien brazos." ILSEU, 11 February, p. 3.
"El niño que no quiso crecer." EU, 10 March, p. 4.
"Palabras sin pasaporte." EU, 2 April, p. 4.
"Saudades." ILSEU, 6 May, p. 4.
"Milagro en Monaco." EU, 8 July, p. 4.
"La doncella-galán." ILEU, 2 October, pp. 4–5.
"Tres sonrisas de mujer." ILEU, 27 November, p. 4.
"El zoo de los poetas." ILEU, 18 December, p. 4.
"El secreto de Dulcinea." EU, 28 December, p. 4.

1959

"El violín de Ingres." ILEU, 5 February, p. 1.
"Los pudores públicos." ILEU, 19 March, p. 3.
"El mar, la mar." ILEU, 23 April, pp. 4–5.

Selected Bibliography 145

"Mi casona y el Rubicón." ILEU, 14 May, p. 6.
"Yo, pecador." EU, 2 June, p. 4.
"Paraíso sin mujer." ILEU, 30 July, p. 3.
"Dos letras, dos mundos." ILEU, 20 August, p. 3.
"Corazón-robot." ILEU, 8 October, p. 6.
"La luna invadida." EU, 16 October, p. 4.
"Naturaleza muerta." ILEU, 10 December, pp. 4–5.

1960
"Allá abajo y allá lejos." ILEU, 14 January, p. 2.
"La edad ideal." ILEU, 4 February, p. 1.
"Vivamos cien años." ILEU, 3 March, p. 6.
"También cumplen años las mujeres." ILEU, 7 April, p. 5.
"La mujer contra el tiempo." ILEU, 19 May, p. 1.
"Coleccionistas de monstruos." ILEU, 9 June, p. 4.
"Lágrimas de ayer." ILEU, 14 July, p. 3.
"Color-pasión," ILEU, 11 August, p. 5.
"Ríos sin mapa." ILEU, 18 August (but dated 25), p. 1.
"Burros y caballos." ILEU, 11 October, p. 1.
"Duendes en los dedos." ILEU, 26 October, p. 1.
"La vista de la anciana dama." ILEU, 15 November, p. 2.
"Dos snobismos." ILEU, 20 December, p. 1.

1961
"De Werther a Eichmann." ILEU, 21 January, p. 1.
"Juan de Juanes." ILEU, 28 February, p. 1.
"El gran desconocido." ILEU, 9 May, p. 2.
"Niñas terribles." ILEU, 25 April, p. 1.
"Teoría del alfiler." ILEU, 30 May, p. 1.
"Y dijo Dios 'Hágase el beso.'" ILEU, 4 July, p. 2.
"Mundo sin beso." ILEU, 18 July, p. 2.
"Coleccionistas de besos." ILEU, 12 September, p. 1.
"El metro, la ironía y la niebla." ILEU, 19 September, p. 1.
"Bajo el signo de Tauro." ILEU, 24 October, p. 1.
"Mitología de bolsillo." ILEU, 21 November, p. 1.

1962
"Se alquila poeta." ILEU, 23 January, p. 1.
"Mujer sonora." ILEU, 27 February, p. 4.
"Los gorriones cantan en prosa." ILEU, 13 March, p. 2.
"Las golondrinas vuelven." ILEU, 3 April, p. 2.
"Lope y las mujeres, I (El primer beso)." ILEU, 24 April, p. 1.
"Lope y las mujeres, II [Dorotea]." ILEU, 29 May, p. 2.
"Lope y las mujeres: Belisa." ILEU, 12 June, p. 1.

"Lope y las mujeres: Lucinda." ILEU, 17 July, p. 1.
"Lope y las mujeres: Juana de Guardo." ILEU, 25 September, p. 2.
"Lope y las mujeres: Jerónima de Burgos." ILEU, 9 October, p. 1.
"Lope y las mujeres: Marta de Nevares." ILEU, 6 November, p. 1.
"¡Feliz viaje, sonrisa!" ET, 22 December, p. 5.
"Lope y las mujeres: Antoñica." LDSET, 30 December, p. 3.

1963
"La rebelión de los robots." ET, 29 January, pp. 4.
"Los concursos de belleza y de poesía." LDSET, 3 March, p. 2.
"Rubia contra morena." LDSET, 28 April, p. 2.
"Escalofón de vanidades." LDSET, 26 May, p. 5.
"Sistema métrico espiritual." ET, 7 July, p. 4.
"Violín gitano." ILEU, 3 September, p. 1.
"¿Dormir? . . . ¿soñar?" LDSET, 6 October, p. 4.
"Sueños en el teatro." ILEU, 15 October, p. 1.

1964
"Calderón ha estrenado anoche." ILEU, 18 February, p. 1.
"Cine contra teatro." LDSET, 19 April, p. 7.
"El poeta y la muerte." ILEU, 21 April, p. 2.
"Las dos ventanas del alma." LDSET, 31 May, p. 1.
"Las coplas de la Police." ILEU, 16 June, p. 4.
"La última isla." ILEU, 11 August, p. 1.
"Literatura mediante." LDSET, 30 August, p. 2.
"Laconismo." LDSET, 15 November, p. 1.

1965
"El jardín de Chopin." EU, 20 January, p. 4.
"Código animal." EU, 11 March, p. 4.
"El anillo y el pez." EU, 12 July, p. 4.

SECONDARY SOURCES

Arias, Manuel Antonio. "Casona, padagogo." *BIEA,* no. 57 (April 1966):73–84. Reviews Casona's contribution to education in Spain, both as a teacher and a writer.

Astur Fernández, Nestor. "Casona en la otra orilla del idioma español." *BIEA*, no. 57 (April 1966):45–60. Presents brief biobibliographic data on Casona in America.

Avello, Manuel. "Recuerdo de Alejandro Casona." *BIEA*, no. 57 (April 1966):61–65. Says his early reading of Casona's *Flor de leyendas* awakened his love of reading in general. Repeats some bibliographic details and introduces Casona's article "Cantares de navidad."

Balseiro, José, and Riis Owre, J. "Introduction" to the school edition of *La barca sin pescador*. New York: Oxford University Press, 1955, pp. xi–xlvii. Presents biographic data and reviews Casona's works in general, with emphasis on *La barca sin pescador*.

―――. "Introduction" to *Corona de amor y muerte*. New York: Oxford University Press, 1960, pp. ix–xxvii. Emphasis on *Corona de amor y muerte*.

Balseiro, José, and Suárez Rivero, Eliana. "Introduction" to the school edition of *El caballero de las espuelas de oro*. New York: Oxford University Press, 1968. Like the preceding "Introductions," of plays edited for intermediate level reading in American universities, this one offers a brief biography and an overview of Casona's works, emphasizing the drama in question.

Bernal Labrada, Hilda. *Simbolo, mito y leyenda en el teatro de Casona*. Oviedo: Instituto de Estudios Asturianos, 1972. Title indicates the direction of commentary. Interesting and valuable, but incomplete.

Bianchi, Alfredo A. "El teatro de Alejandro Casona." *Nosotros* June 1936, pp. 309–14. One of the early commentaries on Casona's theater. Praises the quality of his work.

BIEA, no. 57 (April 1966). The entire number is dedicated to Alejandro Casona. It contains articles by Victoriano Rivas André, Manuel Ruiz Lagos, Néstor Astur Fernández, Manuel F. Avello, Alejandro Casona, Manuel Antonio Arias, Luciano Castañón, Antonio García Miñor, Angeles Arango, Juan Santana, Adela Palacio, and José Rodríguez Richart.

Borras, Angel A. "Musical Underscoring in the Dramas of Casona." *Hispania* 47, no. 3 (September 1964):507–9. Examines Casona's use of music to create particular dramatic effects.

Caso González, José. "Fantasía y realidad en el teatro de Alejandro Casona." *Archivum* 5, no. 2 and 3 (1955):304–18. Early commentary on Casona's tendency to blend fantasy and reality in his plays.

Doménech, Ricardo. "Crítica a *La dama del alba*." *Primer Acto*, no. 34 (May 1962).

_____. "Crítica a *La barca sin pescador.*" *Primer Acto,* no. 41 (March 1963).
_____. "Crítica a *Los árboles mueren de pie.*" *Primer Acto,* no. 49 (January 1964).
_____. "Para un arreglo de cuentas con el teatro de Casona." *Insula,* April 1964.
_____. "Crítica a *Prohibido suicidarse en primavera.*" *Primer Acto,* no. 63 (April 1965). All of these critiques and commentaries by Doménech are an overt, unobjective rejection of Casona's theater in general.
Dulsey, Bernard. "An Afternoon with Casona." *Hispania* 47 (March 1960):79-81. Reviews a chat with Casona wherein are suggested some of Casona's views on Tennessee Williams, Arthur Miller, Calderón, Lope, and censorship. Superficial.
_____. "Casona como crítico." *Hispanófila,* no. 26 (1966):46-51. Uses the format of a question/answer interview to tap Casona's views on modern theater in America, France, England, Latin America, Spain; and on tragedy, comedy, etc. Brief and superficial, but interesting.
Entrambasaguas, Joaquín de. "El teatro de Alejandro Casona." *Clavileño,* July-August 1950, pp. 34-35. A sympathetic commentary on Casona's theater that advocates, but does not provide, a detailed analysis of his plays.
Fernández Santos, A. "Diez comentarios a un año de teatro en Madrid." *Primer Acto,* no. 48 (December 1963).
_____. "Textos para una historia del teatro español." *Primer Acto,* no. 49 (January 1964).
_____. "La vuelta de García Lorca." *Primer Acto,* no. 50 (February 1964).
_____. "Alejandro Casona." *Primer Acto,* no. 68 (1965). All criticism by Fernández Santos represents some degree of negation relative to Casona, but the last (no. 68) is vituperative, unobjective, ungentlemanly, and critically unacceptable.
García Miñor, Antonio. "Alejandro Casona." *BIEA,* no. 57 (April 1966):89-106. Author uses Casona's sister Matutina as his principal reference point to review, nostalgically, Casona's boyhood and subsequent development as a playwright.
Gillespie, Ruth C. "Introduction" to *La sirena varada.* New York: Appleton Century Crofts, 1951, pp. v-xviii. Among the earliest school editions of one of Casona's works to appear in this country.
Gurza, Esperanza. *La realidad caleidoscópica de Alejandro Casona.* Oviedo: Editorial I.D.E.A., 1968. The author examines the multiple "realities" of Casona's plays—the reality of fantasy, of illusion, of dreams, of love, etc.
Keats, Laurence W. "Mysterious Miraculous Mandarin." *Revue de*

Littérature Comparée 40 (1966):497–525. Deals with Eça de Queiroz's Mandarin theme. On pp. 517–19 he specifically treats *La barca sin pescador*. Ignoring the play's traditional roots, he is caustically negative.

Leighton, Charles H. "Alejandro Casona and the New Theater in Spain." Unpublished doctoral dissertation, Harvard University, 1961. Thorough, insightful, and valuable commentary on Casona's life and works up to 1960.

———. "Alejandro Casona and the Revolt against Reason." *Modern Language Journal* 46 (1962):56–61. Shows how Casona's theater represents a positive reaction to the existential crisis as opposed to existentialism, which represents a negative one. Excellent.

———. "Alejandro Casona and the Significance of Dreams." *Hispania* 45 (1962):697–703. Covers Casona's preoccupation with dreams. Traces Freudian and Jungian influences in Casona's thought.

———. "Alejandro Casona's Pirandellism." *Symposium* 17 (1963):202–14. Compares Casona's theater with Pirandello's, showing that Casona largely rejects both the Pirandellian theses and the Pirandellian solution.

———. "Alejandro Casona y las ideas." *Insula*, no. 206 (January 1964):5. Leighton summarizes his views on Casona's position in twentieth-century thought and ideas.

———. "Casona and Lorca: A Brief Comparison." *Modern Drama* 7 (1964):28–34. "Casona is to Lorca what [Oscar] Wilde was to [John Millington] Synge." An excellent comparison of the two authors' works.

———. "Alejandro Casona and the Devil." *Hispania* 48 (1965):29–36. Traces Casona's interest in and treatment of the Devil, academically and theatrically.

———. "Alejandro Casona as Essayist: The Message Finds Its Medium." *Revista de Estudios Hispánicos* 6, no. 1 (January 1972):97–120. Excellent coverage of Casona's ideology as expressed in his essays and implied in his plays.

———. "Alejandro Casona and Suicide." *Hispania* 55, no. 3 (1972):463–65. Examines Casona's preoccupation with self-destruction and analyzes his beliefs concerning suicide in terms of their compatibility with Freudian doctrine.

———. "Casona, Matrism, and La razón Vital." *Hispanófila*, no. 52 (September 1974):35–43. Shows clear parallels between Casona and Ortega, and affirms Casona's matristic ideology.

Monleón, José. "Alejandro Casona frente a su teatro." *Primer Acto*, no. 49 (January 1964).

———. "Un año de teatro subvencionado." *Primer Acto*, no. 62 (March 1964).

———. "Nuestra Natacha hoy." *Triunfo*, no. 91 (January 29, 1966).

———. "Treinta años de teatro de la derecha." *Triunfo,* no. 400 (January 31, 1970).
———. "Mientras arde el mundo." *Triunfo,* no. 401 (February 7, 1970).
———. "El crepúsculo de un premio Nobel." *Triunfo,* no. 402 (February 21, 1970).
———. "Ni los unos ni los otros sino todo lo contrario." *Triunfo,* no. 404 (February 28, 1970).
———. "Pacto y libertad o bienvenidos a casa." *Triunfo,* no. 406 (March 14, 1970). Monleón struggles for objectivity in his criticism of Casona. Though he remains negative, he is at least a gentleman.

Moon, Harold K. "Calderón and Casona." *Hispania* 48 (March 1965):31–42. Traces similarities between Calderón and Casona, and especially between *La vida es sueño* and *La tercera palabra.*

———. "Alejandro Casona and Henri Bergson." In *Spanish Thought and Letters in the Twentieth Century.* Edited by Germán Bleiberg and E. Inman Fox, pp. 345–59. Nashville: Vanderbilt University Press, 1966. Shows parallels between Bergson and Casona.

———. "Death in the Theater of Alejandro Casona." *Brigham Young University Studies* 10 (Autumn 1969):107–17. Touches upon Casona's ideology regarding death, but mostly traces the qualities of Casona's *Peregrina* as she blends allegory and human warmth.

———. *Alejandro Casona, Playwright.* Provo, Utah: Merrill Monograph Series, BYU Press, 1970. General commentary on Casona's life and works; a prelude to the present book.

———. " 'Love More Powerful Than Death'; Mystic Resonances in *Corona de amor y muerte."* *Rocky Mountain Review of Language and Literature* 32, no. 1 (Winter 1978):47–56. Shows the Christian symbolism, with suggestions of mysticism, in *Corona de amor y muerte.*

Newberry, Wilma. *The Pirandellian Mode in Spanish Literature from Cervantes to Sastre.* Albany: State University of New York Press, 1973. In her chapter on Casona (pp. 145–50), Newberry repeats essentially the same data advanced by Charles H. Leighton in "Alejandro Casona's Pirandellism," adding some commentary on *Los árboles mueren de pie,* already covered in *Alejandro Casona, Playwright.*

Palacio Gross, Adela. "Casona y la crítica actual." *BIEA,* April 1966, pp. 115–46. Reviews the negative criticism of Casona that appeared over a determined period in *Primer Acto,* showing that it is largely unobjective, unfair, and often vituperative.

Plans, Juan José. *Alejandro Casona.* Oviedo: Richard Grandío, 1965. A very interesting, deeply personal and rewarding biographic

Selected Bibliography

treatment of Casona. Plans presents both sides of the critical crossfire concerning Casona, but is obviously sympathetic.

Rivas, Andre Victoriano. "Actitud social en el teatro de Casona." *Reseña*, December 1965, pp. 343–47. Title indicates the thrust of this article.

———. "Notas para una voloración del teatro de Casona." *Reseña*, February 1966, pp. 145–56.

———. "Poesía y angustia en el teatro de Casona." *BIEA*, April 1966, pp. 3–28. Catalogs the types of fantasy in Casona's works and affirms that Casona's plays, if properly understood, are *not* evasionist.

Rodríguez-Castellano, Juan. "Alejandro Casona expatriado español." *Hispania* 25 (February 1942):49–54. Affirms Casona's loyalty to his homeland.

———. "Introduction" to the edition of *La dama del alba*. New York: Charles Scribner's Sons, 1947, pp. xi–xx. This edition appears the same year as Shoemaker's edition of *Nuestra Natacha*. These are the first school editions of Casona's works to appear in this country. The "Introduction" covers Casona's life and works, emphasizing *La dama del alba*. Also contains an appendix that explains customs and legends of Asturias.

———. "Casona y Asturias." *Hispania* 35 (August 1952):392–94. As the title suggests, the article examines the influence of Asturias in Casona's theater.

———. "Introduction" to *Los árboles mueren de pie*. New York: Henry Holt, 1953, pp. ix–xxiii. Similar in purpose and scope to his edition of *La dama del alba*.

———. "Doctrinas pedagógicas de Alejandro Casona." *Hispania*, no. 3 (March 1960):25–29. Traces Casona's pedagogical views through his theater and points up the playwright's basic optimism.

———. "Mi última conversación con Alejandro Casona." *Revista de Estudios Hispánicos* 1 (1967):183–93. The author recounts his conversation with Casona just prior to the latter's death. What is of greatest interest here is Casona's response to ten questions that Rodríguez Castellano put to him relative to current topics.

Rodríguez Richart, José. *Vida y teatro de Alejandro Casona*. Oviedo: Instituto de Estudios Asturianos, 1963. An excellent, thorough treatment of Casona's biography and works.

———. "Imaginación y realismo en el teatro: *La Barca sin pescador* de Casona." *Boletín de la biblioteca Menéndez Pelayo* 39 (1963):235–51. Defends Casona against some obtuse allegations by an individual whose eagerness to hop on the "engagé" bandwagon far outdistanced his ability as a critic.

———. "Casona y Norteamérica." *BIEA*, April 1966, pp. 147–203.

While proposing to deal with the works of Casona edited in this country, and especially with the introductions by the editors of those works, Rodríguez Richart rambles through many interesting and valid topics relative to Casona's theater. Well worth the reading.

Rogers, Elizabeth S. "Multiple Doubling in *La dama del alba.*" A paper read at the Conference on Film and Comparative Literature, Florida State University, January 25, 1980. Makes the important point that, symbolically, Angélica and Adela in *La dama del alba* are one and the same—*doubles,* with Adela the redeemed version of the fallen Angélica.

———. "Casona and López Rubio: Theater as Real as Life." *Rocky Mountain Review of Language and Literature* 34, no. 2 (Spring 1980):136–49. Examines one of Casona's plays (*Los árboles mueren de pie*) and one of López Rubio's (*La venda en los ojos*) in the light of role-playing to perceive the relationship between illusion and reality in both authors' works. A slightly new twist on an old theme.

Ruiz-Lagos, Manuel. "La voz impersonal: Una técnica dramática de Alejandro Casona." *BIEA,* April 1966, pp. 29–44. Explicates a technique that achieves universality for Casona's plays. Though the author himself does not mention it, his *voz impersonal* recalls the sententiousness in Lope's *Fuente Ovejuna,* as explained by R. D. F. Pring-Mill, *TDR* 7 (1962):5–37.

Ruiz Ramón, Francisco. "Casona (1903–1965)." In *Historia del teatro español, Siglo XX, II.* Madrid: Alianza Editorial, 1971, pp. 245–69. A very thorough coverage of Casona. Ultimately, Ruiz Ramón sides with the modern "engagés" who reject Casona's theater.

Sainz de Robles, Federico C. "Prologue" of the *Obras Completas de Alejandro Casona.* 6th ed. Madrid: Aguilar, 1967, 1:xi–ccxliv. Excellent coverage of Casona's works, play by play. Indispensable reading for serious students of Casona.

Santana, Juan. "Maestro y misionero." *BIEA,* April 1966, pp. 111–14. Brings to light a publication by Casona that most collectors of Casoniana have overlooked, i.e., "Una misión." Writes of Casona's work with *Misiones Pedagógicas,* particularly in Sanabria.

Schwarz, Kessel. "Reality in the Works of Alejandro Casona." *Hispania* 40 (March 1957):57–61. Affirms that Casona continues the traditional theme of illusion versus reality, characteristic especially of Cervantes and Calderón, and concludes that, on the whole, for Casona the worlds of reality and happiness are synonymous.

Shoemaker, William H. "Introduction" to *Nuestra Natacha.* New York: Appleton Century Crofts, 1947, pp. xi–xxxv. A very good introduction. Includes the usual biographic sketch and general commentary on Casona's works, with emphasis on *Nuestra Natacha*. Also includes a brief bibliography, one of the first compiled on Casona.

Toms, J. Frank. "The Reality-Fantasy Technique of Alejandro Casona." *Hispania* 44 (May 1961):218–21. Discusses Casona's dramatic techniques in presenting the fantasy-reality conflicts so prevalent in his plays.

Torrente Ballestar, Gonzalo. "Teatro de evasión." In *Teatro español contemporáneo*. Madrid: Ediciones Guadarrama, 1957, pp. 205–8. Sympathetic but superficial coverage of Casona, typical of most literary histories. Includes Casona in the "evasionist" group of dramatists.

Valbuena Prat, Angel. "El teatro novocentista de Alejandro Casona." In *Historia del teatro español*. Barcelona: Editorial Noguer, 1956, pp. 651–56. Sympathetic but not penetrating coverage of Casona's theater.

Woolsey, Wallace A. "Illusion versus Reality in Some of the Plays of Alejandro Casona." *Modern Language Journal* 38 (1954):80–84. More on the typical illusion-reality conflict, with a conclusion too rigid and too sweeping: "An illusory or imaginary way of life must fade away in the pitiless light of reality."

Index

Adamuz, Anita, 3
Alarcón, Pedro A. de, 18, 28–40;
  El sombrero de tres picos, 18, 28–40
Artigas, Santiago, 7
Astrana Marín, Luis, 122–23
Avila, Francisco de, 20

Bartolomé Cossío, Manuel, 8
Balseiro, José, 6, 13–15, 20, 25–26, 109
Benavente, Jacinto, 25, 76
Bentley, Eric, 85–86
Berceo, Gonzalo de, 57
Bergson, Henri, 34, 45, 46, 48, 91, 92, 96, 130
Blair, Walter, 50
Boccaccio, Giovanni: *Decamerone*, 20, 27

Caçao de amigo, 119
Calderón de la Barca, Pedro, 3, 21, 27, 42; *La vida es sueño*, 3, 21, 22; *El mágico prodigioso*, 42
Caso González, José, 18
Casona, Alejandro: birth and early childhood, 1–3; formative years, 3–6; young manhood and early profession as teacher, 6–8; beginnings of theatrical career, 8–10; Patronato de Misiones Pedagógicas and the Teatro del Pueblo, 8–10; theatrical success, 10–13; wins Lope de Vega prize with *La sirena varada*, 11; exile and wandering, 13–15; refuge in Argentina,

Casona, Alejandro (*continued*)
  15–16; accused of plagiarism, 16–17; work in motion picture industry, 17; pinnacle of success, 19–24; return to Spain, 24–25; death, 25–26

WORKS:
A Belén, pastores, 20, 40, 42
árboles mueren de pie, Los, 19, 20, 79–82, 86–88, 91–92, 129
barca sin pescador, La, 18, 25, 40, 49–66, 98, 130
caballero de las espuelas de oro, El, 25, 105, 119–27, 130
Carta de una desconocida, 23
casa de los siete balcones, La, 23, 74–75, 98, 102–104
"casa del amor, La," 115
Celestina, La, 25, 26, 130
Corona de amor y muerte, 22–23, 27, 105–19, 130
crimen de Lord Arturo, El, 11, 14, 98
dama del alba, La, 17, 18, 25, 66–75
"Diablo en la literatura y el arte, El," 6, 40
"Don Juan el el Diablo," 45
entremés del mancebo que casó con mujer brava, El, 10
flauta del sapo, La, 7
Flor de leyendas, 10, 27
llave en el desván, La, 20, 98–104
María Curie, 16
misterio de María Celeste, El, 11

Index

Casona, Alejandro (*continued*)
  WORKS (*continued*)
    molinera de Arcos, La, 18, 19, 28–40, 45, 130
    Novelas selectas de Voltaire, 6
    Nuestra Natacha, 12, 13, 15
    Otra vez el Diablo, 6, 10, 12, 40–49, 52, 130
    peregrina de la barba florida, La, 5
    Prohibido suicidarse en primavera, 14, 82–85, 92, 96, 129
    Retablo jovial, 20, 27
    Romance de Dan y Elsa, 14, 15
    Sancho Panza en la isla, 10
    Siete gritos en el mar, 20, 21, 98–99, 103–104, 130
    Sinfonía inacabada, 15, 105
    sirena varada, La, 7, 10, 11, 12, 15, 17, 25, 77–79, 89–91, 129
    tercera palabra, La, 21–22, 98
    Tres diamantes y una mujer, 23–24
    tres perfectas casadas, Las, 16–17, 25
    "Tres sonrisas de mujer," 14
    "Yo, pecador," 41–42

Castro, Inés de, 22, 105–19
Cervantes, Miguel de, 10, 27, 76; *Don Quijote de la Mancha,* 10, 27
Charlemagne, 5
Chateaubriand, François René de, 18, 115
Cobos, Pedro de, 68
Coleridge, Samuel Taylor, 57–59
Collado, Manuel, 14
"Comedy of Forgiveness," 56–66
Criticism and Casona's ideological context in *La barca sin pescador,* 53–61

Darío, Rubén, 5; *Portico,* 5
De Quincey, Thomas: *Confessions of an English Opium Eater,* 6
Díaz-Collado Co., 14, 15, 18, 20
Díaz, Josefina, 7
Díaz, Pepita, 14
Díaz Rengifo, Juan, 20
Doménech, Ricardo, 54
Dramatic techniques in *Corona de amor y muerte,* 109–19

Eliade, Mircea, 55
Elina Colmar-Carlos Cores Co., 22
Entrambasaguas, Joaquín de, 52, 68
Evreinov, Nicolai, 82, 84; *The Foundation of Happiness,* 82; *The Chief Thing,* 82

Falangistas, 13
Fernández de Castro, Pedro, 107
Fernández de Moratín, Leandro, 10
Foster, Jerald R., 115
Freud, Sigmund, 96, 98, 115
Fromm, Erich, 96
Frye, Northrop, 59, 63

Garber, Eugene, 50
García Lorca, Federico, 96, 115
Gerber, John, 50
Ginastero, Alberto, 24; *Don Rodrigo,* 24
Giner de los Ríos, Francisco, 8
Gómez Tejada de los Reyes, Cosme, 20
Góngora, Luis de, 20, 120
Gracián, Baltasar, 22, 66, 128; *El criticón,* 22
Grammatica, Emma, 19
Gurza, Esperanza, 117–18

Heim, Elsa, 19
Heine, Heinrich, 10

Hernández Catá, 11
Historical Background for *El caballero de las espuelas de oro*, 122–24

Jara Carrillo, Pedro, 4
Johnson, Samuel, 57–59
Juan Manuel, Infante Don: *El conde Lucanor*, 10, 27, 107

Keats, L. W., 58

Ladrón de Guevarra-Rivello, 7
Leibniz, Gottfried Wilhelm, 22
Leighton, Charles H., 21, 24, 27, 54–55, 76, 78, 85, 96, 114, 129
Leon, Luis de, 7
Llovet, Enrique, 25
López, Fernán(do), 22, 108

Machado, Manuel, 5, 27
MacLeish, Archibald: *Ars Poetica*, 57
Madrid, Francisco, 16
Manso, Pedro, 122
Marquina, Eduardo, 5
Martínez Sierra, Gregorio: *Canción de cuna*, 3
Mecha Díaz Co., 14
Melía-Cibrián Co., 17
Membrives, Lola, 17
Mira de Amescua, Antonio: *El esclavo del demonio*, 42
Molière: *Le Medecin malgré lui*, 10; *Les Precieuses ridicules*, 31

Narvaez, Pacheco de, 120, 123

Ocaña, Francisco, 20
Overstreet, Harry Allen, 92
Owre, J. Riis, 6, 13, 109

Papini, Giovanni, 41–42, 128
Pérez Galdós, Benito, 3, 13, 24, 124, 125; *Electra*, 13; *La loca de la casa*, 3
Pirandello, Luigi, 76, 79, 85–86, 96; *Enrico IV (Henry IV)*, 86; *Il piacere dell' onestà (The Pleasure of Honesty)*, 86
Plans, José, 3, 5, 8, 54
Ponce de Leon, Luis, 54–55

Queiroz, Eça de, 18, 61; *O Mandarim*, 18
Quevedo, Francisco de, 119–27, 130; *Suenos*, 121

Reichenberger, Arnold, 55
Reisman, David, et al: *The Lonely Crowd*, 54
Rodríguez Alvarez, Alejandro. See Casona, Alejandro
Rodríguez Castellano, Juan, 21, 67, 82
Rodríguez Richart, José, 4, 5, 7, 15, 16, 53–54, 113
Rojas, Fernando de, 26
Romance del palmero, 119
Rostand, Edmond: *Cyrano de Bergerac*, 124–26
Rousseau, Jean Jacque, 18, 61
Ruis de Alarcón, Juan, 120
Ruiz Ramón, Francisco, 54, 58

Sainz de Robles, Federico Carlos, 3, 14, 19, 21–22, 23, 27, 35, 42, 52
Saudades, 57
Schnitzler, Arthur: *Der tod des Junggeseller*, 16–17
Seneca, 74
Shakespeare, William, 57–66; *All's Well That Ends Well*, 57; *Measure for Measure*, 57, 58

Index

Shoemaker, William H., 3, 9, 11, 12–13
Singerman, Berta, 23
Soares de Valladares, Aldonza, 107
Socrates, 85, 129
Souviron, José María, 7
Strindberg, August, 7
Suárez, Constantino, 7, 8, 10
Suárez Rivero, Eliana, 25–26

Tiempo, César, 2
Teresa de Jesús, 118

Valle Inclán, Ramón del, 6
Vega, Lope Félix de, 20, 108, 120, 121; *El ansuelo de Fenisa,* 23

Vehil-Cerrador Co., 20
Vehil, Luisa, 23
Vélez de Guevara, Luis, 42, 108; *El diablo cojuelo,* 42; *Reinar después de morir,* 108
Velloso, J. M., 53
Voltaire, 6; *Candide,* 22

Wheelwright, Philip, 40
Wilde, Oscar, 7, 14; *The Crime of Lord Arthur of Savile,* 7

Xirgú-Borrás Co., 10, 11
Xirgú, Margarita, 14, 17

Zamacois, Eduardo, 2
Zweig, Stefan, 23

THE LIBRARY
ST. MARY'S COLLEGE OF MARYLAND
ST. MARY'S CITY, MARYLAND 20686